Father Bede's Misfit

Phil H. Troyer

York Press   Parkton, Maryland

Published by York Press, Inc.,
Parkton, Maryland 21120.
Manufactured in the United States of America.
Typeset by Brushwood Graphics Studio,
Baltimore, Maryland.
Printed by The Maple Press Co.,
York, Pennsylvania
Cover and jacket design by Joseph Dieter, Jr.
Jacket illustration by Nancy Johnston.

Library of Congress Catalog Card Number
86–050533.

ISBN   0–912752–11–4

**While the characters in this book are based on
real people, all effort has been made to protect
their privacy by changing names and locales.**

ACKNOWLEDGMENTS

"I Saw the Light" by Hank Williams. © 1948 by Fred Rose Music, Inc.
Copyright renewed. Assigned to Fred Rose Music, Inc. and Aberbach En-
terprises, Ltd. (Rightsong Music, Administrator) for the U.S.A. only. All
rights outside the U.S.A. controlled by Fred Rose Music, Inc. International
Copyright Secured. ALL RIGHTS RESERVED. Used by permission.
"Five Feet High and Rising" by Johnny Cash. © 1959 by Johnny Cash
Music, Inc. All rights controlled by Unichappell Music, Inc. (Rightsong
Music, Publisher). ALL RIGHTS RESERVED. Used by permission.
"Honky Honkin' " by Hank Williams. © 1948 by Fred Rose Music, Inc.
Copyright renewed. Assigned to Fred Rose Music, Inc. and Aberbach En-
terprises, Ltd. (Rightsong Music, Administrator) for the U.S.A. only. All
rights outside the U.S.A. controlled by Milene Music, Inc. ALL RIGHTS
RESERVED. Used by permission.

To My Father and Mother

Good comes out of bad when you find a friend in an unexpected haven

It is a crisp fall day, two weeks to the day since I came to the monastery. Father Bede in his tattered corduroy coat is behind the wheel of my old Chevy. Deaf Don's corn bread and coffee in our bellies and the gates of the monastery still squeaking on their hinges, we barrel noisily down the middle of the narrow mountain road on the way to Laro, the back seat loaded to the window ledge with old clothes and mended toys for the poor Spanish families. Father Bede is singing at the top of his ragged crew cut above the racket of the leaky muffler: "Oh you can't get to heaven in an old Chev-ee, an old Chev-ee, an old . . ." I brake against the floorboards with both feet as we swing into a blind curve.

Mesas rise starkly on the far-away horizon; behind us in the rearview mirror are the snow-capped Guadalupe Mountains. The beaded hippies and flower children have not arrived yet. Neither have the Winnebagoes, trail bikes, campers, and customized vans.

1

When we get to Laro, children on their way to school race after us shouting and waving. Father slows, sticks his head out of the window, leans on the horn, and waves wildly.

We stop for gas. Two mongrels, all hip bone and rib cage, sniff each other as they go around in a circle. Father jumps out to egg them on. He whistles shrilly through his teeth, claps his hands, and shouts, "Get 'em, sic 'em, sic 'em." The dogs snarl and growl, and then they're on each other tooth and fur. Father springs up onto the trunk of my car to keep out of the way and whoops them on: "Get 'em boy, that's it, bite 'em, sic 'em good."

I sit there not quite sure what to make of it, but enjoying myself. I just hope there won't be any new dents in my trunk lid.

We climb a winding dirt road to the top of the village, where we will distribute the cartons of clothes and toys. Smoke is curling from the chimneys of the little adobe houses, scattered in clusters on the hillsides, with strings of bright red and green chili peppers hanging from their door latches. The sky is clear and deep blue and the adobe houses are bathed in the sun's light.

Father Bede whoops, "Bill, Bill, you and I are just two pebbles on the beach, but God will pick us up and throw us at the Devil."

Today, years later, Father Bede has left the order and is a parish priest in some small southern town. Father Burkhart is dead of a heart attack. Brother Vincent, the farmboy from Nebraska, died recently while helping the poor in Central America. Brother Patrick is a cowpoke on a ranch in Utah, or so I've been told.

God only knows where Brother Frank is. Father Bede was his friend, as he was mine, and he tried to help Frank, but maybe Frank couldn't be helped. The rumors are that he is impersonating a priest and even says Mass. Perhaps he is still wearing the clerical collar he stole from Father Burkhart.

I don't know why I ended up at the monastery at Laro. My having known all of them was probably just chance. Or was there something to what Father Bede told me the morning after I arrived?

"God gives us free will. He doesn't tell us what to do. He doesn't make us do good, or prevent us from doing evil. But sometimes, when it's to serve a special purpose, He intervenes in our lives."

Father Bede talked on about Causality and Divine Providence. Cause and effect are, he said, like a game of dominoes; each domino knocks over the next, each event determines the next one, and so on down the line. "I believe it was determined since you were a small boy, perhaps before that, that someday you would come to the monastery."

I didn't really think God had brought me to the monastery, but no one had ever taken the interest in me that Father Bede did.

Quitting, giving up, getting out, that's a relief, a step out of difficulties

The road to Laro had been a long one and deathly lonely. When, after a summer as a bellboy in a Denver hotel, I called my parents to tell them that I was not coming back to college, that I was quitting after three semesters, that I was on my own, I felt their deep disappointment and alarm sagging the wire.

"I wanted to be a good student," I told them. "I worked like hell and I did the absolute best I could, but all I could do was scrape bottom. I can't remember anything I read. I can't keep up taking lecture notes. I can't remember anything. I'm dumber than I can stand being, and don't tell me I'm running myself down. I'm sorry. Please don't worry about me."

In our family, not to complete your college education was tantamount to failure, and although I tried to tell myself it wasn't true, I felt a desperate sense of loss and giving up. I worked hard, only to achieve mediocrity, and that wasn't enough reward. And I felt too much fear of and anger toward the other students and some of my professors. I could make nothing—school, jobs, or friendships—work for me.

My father, who loved me, was desperate to help me during my freshman year, not knowing quite how: "You have some kind of itch to get away. You're lonely, desperate, afraid of people. You're a frightened, spindly-faced kid, nervous, high-strung, like a poodle dog wiggling its stub of a tail. You're too shy to say your own name. If someone crooks a finger at you, you run in the opposite direction. You want to get away from people, you want to go hide in a dark, empty back room like a mouse."

I had done poorly in school from the first grade on. I couldn't grasp what other children my age were expected to do and did easily: Follow directions, learn the alphabet, memorize the multiplication tables. In the second grade I could barely count on my fingers. In the third grade I still did not know the names of many of the colors. Words on a page sprang out at me in a jumble like the gears and spring of an alarm clock I took apart. Exasperated by my inability to catch on and by what they took to be my attitude of not trying, I was more than once physically shaken by teachers. Some of the kids brought seamtresses' tapes to school to measure my head to see if there was enough room for brains. I was withdrawn and preoccupied, a daydreamer, my report card said. I was held back a grade.

From the beginning, defeat, frustration, and fear created a pattern of passivity, timidity, and uncertainty, making me the object of classroom titters and neighborhood bullies.

Continuing our phone conversation, my father had asked, "Does this mean that you're giving up entirely on your education?" He had given up on me. "Well, O.K., if your mind's made up, perhaps we'd better just say good-bye, good luck, and take care."

I had thrown my clothes in the back seat of my Chevy, and a

few minutes later I was headed out of Denver. I spent the night at the Y.M.C.A. in Colorado Springs. TV's blared, radios played nonstop at full volume, an old man next door played polkas on his concertina and stamped his foot, doors were slammed violently, several men talked thoughtlessly and endlessly at the tops of their voices out in the hallway during the early morning hours, and at daybreak the maid burst into the room with her pass key after only a cursory rap that didn't give me time to respond, catching me in my underpants. The noise and intrusion infuriated me. I felt desperate.

After a sleepless night I felt an urge to drive south through New Mexico, as far as a day or two of driving would take me, feeling despair, yet a kind of exhilaration. I wanted to see the desert. I felt drawn to the quiet and solitude. I had some tip money I'd saved and I could get by on very little food. I wanted to get the hotel out of my guts, and get as far away from people and noise as I could. I started out about noon.

South of Pueblo my car floated through immense oceans of bluish bunchgrass as tall as an Iowa cornfield, stretching to the horizon and swallowing my car and the road. I had never seen anything like it and I looked at the face of a driver, who was passing in the opposite direction on the flat, endless stretch of otherwise empty highway, to see if he was as astonished as I was.

Soon the four-lane highway vanished and I rolled along on a narrow old concrete road without berm, grass growing up through the cracks, lost in the desolate prairie flatland.

There were no trees, farmhouses, or fences, only a straight and endless row of telephone poles without crossbars reaching to the horizon, each pole stark and blunt. A few cattle in the faraway distance looked like dark, immobile specks and once in a great while there was a forlorn, abandoned, tenant-farmer's shack, or an aban-doned motel, boxed in by brush blown there by the wind. Scattered here and there lay the ugly hulls of shredded, recapped truck tires. Balls of tumbleweed drifted across the empty road, rose, fell, and rolled on as if they had a life of their own.

Hours later, crossing the Colorado border and continuing southward, I saw stark mesas rising from the flat desert floor, thousands of feet high, their sheer sides topped with flat crowns. The land was in soft shadows, but the late-afternoon autumn sunlight illuminated the western walls of the mesas, giving them a warm, reddish hue, making every crease and crevice brilliantly clear.

I spent that night in a cheap hotel in Ft. Sumner, New Mexico ('A Home In Every Room'), the dresser drawer full of empty half pints. Falling asleep, dreaming about home and family, I woke up suddenly not knowing where I was, aching with homesickness and feeling utterly alone.

I started out at daybreak before the sleep was out of my eyes. The prairie had long ago faded into desert, vast open spaces of sagebrush and sand, and arroyas into which a man could wander, get turned around, and lose himself forever. Here and there were bright fall flowers, red, purple, and yellow. Water puddle mirages vanished as my car reached them. Sky and earth lay belly to belly as far as the eye could see in any direction, and puffs of diesel smoke appeared on the horizon long before the truck came into view. The highway was empty, and I felt bathed in the warmth of the sun reflected through the windows.

Engulfed in space, I felt a strange feeling of aloneness and separation; my hands gripping the steering wheel seemed detached from my body.

On a deserted stretch of highway fifty miles or more from the nearest city, I was jarred back to earth by a sickening clanking in the engine as my car began to lose compression.

Disbelieving, a vision of my car abandoned forever by the desert roadside, I coasted for a quarter of a mile to a boarded-up and seemingly abandoned, tumble-down tavern with chickens clucking around the gas pump, the only building I'd seen in fifteen miles. Half a dozen Spanish men fluttered out of nowhere like pigeons and gathered around my car. They were unsteady on their feet, and they laughed and pointed at the smoke pouring out from under the hood.

I was half afraid to get out of the car. "Your car's no good, man," said a stocky young man. He leaned through the window on his elbows and stuck his face close to mine. His breath smelled strongly of whiskey on a stomach that hadn't been fed.

"No," I agreed.

An older man stepped up. "I have a friend who fixes cars. Maybe he will fix yours."

That sounded fishy. "Is he a mechanic? Does he have a garage?"

"No, he don't have no garage," he said, grinning and shaking his head. "It's just his hobby."

Were they planning a trap? Or did he really have a friend who fixes cars? I told him I'd call a garage in Carlsbad.

"That's miles from here. It'll cost you a lot of money." Then he offered to tow me to his friend's place for $10.00, and I told him it was too much.

"Nine-fifty," he said laughing, and the others joined in. "Take it or leave it, I don't give a shit."

Apprehensive, I told him I'd take the tow, feeling I had no choice.

With my car in tow behind his pickup, we crossed the highway onto a rough dirt road and jerked along noisily bumper to bumper, like two mating cicadas, my anxiety increasing by the minute, until we reached the edge of a little Spanish settlement called Laro. We turned west, and several miles beyond we stopped in front of an isolated cinderblock house on the edge of the desert. There were a few wrecked cars in the yard, but there was no one around, and it did not look to me like a place where you could have a car fixed.

I went to the door. There were no clothes on the clothesline, the porch was empty, and there were no children's toys in the yard. The man had already unhooked my car, turned his truck around, and was gunning the motor impatiently.

"There's no one here!" I yelled.

"He'll be back! I don't know where he is. Give me my money." And off he went.

I sat there, despairing, in a ton-and-a-half of car that wouldn't budge, and waited. By sundown, six hours later, the owner arrived. He was not Spanish, but Anglo, a huge man, friendly, with a rugged, weathered face, cowboy hat and jeans, and cigar. "I'm sorry you had to wait," he said. "I was in Carlsbad getting parts." He looked my car over and shook his head. "I'll tear it down and see what's wrong with it."

I told him I only had forty-five dollars to spare and he said that would cover it. He told me to come back in two days. Then I walked three miles back down the road to Alejandro's, a little adobe tavern not far from Laro.

I walked in nervously and sat down at the bar, not knowing whether I would be welcome. There were no Anglos in the bar, only seven or eight Spanish men, dark, tough-looking. They all turned around and looked at me. I had $4.00 left for a hotel room that night, and 20¢; I bought a 15¢ glass of beer and sat there drinking it slowly, wary of the staring eyes of the men around me. Leaving Denver, I had felt free and on my own. And here I was a thousand miles from home, angry at my luck, angry at myself, my car broken down, my money gone, not knowing where to spend the night, and in a Spanish bar where I felt I wasn't wanted.

I asked the bartender, a wiry little Spaniard with a hard-eyed steady gaze and scar tissue like crow's feet on his chin and forehead, if there was a hotel in Laro.

"Shit, there isn't no hotels around *here*. Nothin' between here and Carlsbad."

He shook his head as he walked away, muttering in Spanish, and some of the men at the bar laughed. The old feeling of always being out of place swept over me.

What would I do now? I wasn't going back to Denver or to that bellhop job, even if I found a way to get there. I had been glad to be rid of the hotel with its transvestites, homosexuals, and middle-aged prostitutes; the sad, lonely, half-crazy old ladies on the residence floor, their hallway littered with trays of dirty dishes and rotting food that hadn't been collected; the "blue-squad" detectives who dropped in for their coffee breaks and entertained themselves by routing a bellhop or bus boy into a room at the back of the kitchen, leeringly questioning him about his sex habits.

As I sat there drinking my beer, I went over and over my last night at the hotel.

The hotel was hosting a hula party in the ballroom for the Star-dusters. Hawaiian music blared from a record player. Middle-aged men, naked except for green cellophane grass skirts, big bellied and with sagging pectorals, guzzled gin-and-fruit-juice punch from glasses inserted in plastic coconuts served by Robin, the banquet bus boy, a lisping, six-foot-five, slim-hipped, full-blooded Navajo, wearing a large straw hat with the brim unraveled, a pair of mammoth yellow-rimmed sunglasses, and a red foot-long plastic comb sticking out of his tight rear pocket.

Mr. Kuh, the nervous assistant night manager, taking guppy puffs on his cigarette, was in a dither: "Oh, dear, those people, they seemed so nice when I talked to them. Now they're running out with all the decor-ations. There they go again," he shrieked, as two barefoot men in grass skirts ran through the lobby and out the door on either end of a twelve-foot prop palm tree.

Heavily made-up and be-wigged "girls" strutted in and out of the ballroom. Old Jake, the custodian, was muttering: "The damn men's room is full of women. Hell, they ain't women, they're faggots, bun-bandits."

Later that night I went to page someone in the bar. As I was leaving, I heard a voice say softly, "Hey, fart." Startled, I jumped like a stray dog dodging spit, looked around and saw a man walking beside me.

"What do you mean by that?" I asked him.

"Want to dance, fart?"

We stood there in the lobby facing each other. He was short and stocky with a thick, round face. He reached over and put a hand on my shoulder. It infuriated me.

In my childhood, though I was hurt and terrified by the threats, taunts, and tittering of the other children, I somehow assumed that I deserved what I got, because of my dumbness and meekness.

In later years, high school and college, wanting to strike back but unable to, I always retreated instead, hating myself for it, and never forgetting an incident.

And now, I could redeem myself once and for all, feel whole again, by smashing the man in his face.

But I stood there paralyzed and speechless. Then I turned around and walked away, full of rage at myself, at the man, and at the world. "Let me know if you change your mind, fart," he called after me.

It is my manner, my extreme shyness, timidity, hesitancy of speech, and the meekness in my voice, which I hate, that attracts them, bastards everywhere. I've encountered them in jobs, in the factory I worked at before I came to Denver, in bars, in restaurants, on the campus, and almost daily here at the hotel. They have a keen sense for fear and weakness in others, and take a joy in unprovoked meanness.

I sat there in the bellboy's quarters feeling the anger build until I could hardly contain it.

The bell gonged for me and I went to the desk, another check-in, a young couple with a child. They were kind, friendly people, but in spite of myself I made them uncomfortable by my nervousness which increased the harder I tried to control it. I wanted to reach out in some small way, show them some gesture of friendliness to reciprocate, but I couldn't.

My mother and father, whom I deeply love, are kind, modest, quiet people. They would rather overlook a wrong or an injustice than be angry or vindictive or carry a grudge. They want me to be the same and it often infuriates me. But we live in different worlds, even while we are living under *the same roof. They don't know about the world of bullies.*

They raised us to be kind, gentle, and considerate of others. I still have those instincts and believe in them, but they can also be a handicap, and make life hell. These instincts can leave you with a skin that's too thin. They can be interpreted as a sign of effeminacy or even homosexuality. They can make you the target of bullies and bastards who see you as a safe and easy mark to prove to themselves their own manhood.

My parents want me back in school. Dad has been an educator all his life. My two brothers, one my twin, the other younger, breeze along academically and socially.

My parents love me and want the best for me and I can't stand disappointing them, but I haven't convinced them of the way I feel, how demoralized and desperate, how angry at myself and others I am.

"One of those goddam hula-skirted assholes bumped into me and spilled gin and pineapple juice down the front of my suit," Mr. Singer, our top boss, shouted in a fury, tossing it at me. "Trousers, too. Run over to the all-night cleaners. I want the damn spots out. Bust ass!" He had a beak like a turkey buzzard and I was his piece of maggoty flesh.

I took his suit to the cleaners. I told the clerk, "He wants the spots out," and added as an afterthought, "He said he wants the pants shortened three inches too, so his son can wear 'em." It was a lie of course, but I knew then that I wasn't going back to the hotel.

I yanked off my clip-on bowtie, threw it in the gutter, went back to my room to pack my bag. That was when I called home to tell my mother and father that I wasn't coming home or back to school.

I took a sip of beer. By tomorrow my money would be gone and I'd have nothing to eat, no place to stay. I needed to get to Carlsbad and find a job. Leaving the hotel had been the same old story: Work a few weeks or days, get mad and quit. For me, jobs were as short-lived as a bug in a bird's beak.

I was a good worker, a hard worker, when I was employed. I always tried to do things to perfection. But I was constantly wary and frightened of the boss and the other employees, maintained my reticence, got very tense, rattled, and made mistakes. I'd try to interpret every word, every look, every gesture, every intonation of speech, every inflection of voice, in fear that it was a criticism of my work or a dislike of me.

So I did my job quickly, conscientiously, and fearfully, in a silent rage, though I was always polite and apologetic on the surface. And ever wary of encounters with bastards.

From the time I got home until I was able to fall asleep at night, I was consumed by rehashing and analyzing every situation I'd felt threatened by that day. Conflict, fear, anger, and suspicion would balloon inside until I couldn't take the pressure; I knew I'd quit or walk off the job again.

I had asked the bartender, who I was aware had been looking at me steadily, how far it was to Carlsbad.

"Thirty miles, and don't try to hitchhike. No one hitchhikes around here and no one picks up hitchhikers. It's not healthy. You could end up with a knife in your ribs."

"Thanks for the warning."

He looked at me and suddenly his eyes showed kindness. "What *are* you doing around here?"

I told him about my plans to see the desert and how my car broke down. "I'll have to find a way to get to Roswell or Carlsbad and try to find some work."

"Where are you going to stay tonight?" he asked.

I told him I'd sleep in my car and he said, "There are gangs of young punks around here: they'll jack your car up tonight and have the tires off so quick you'll sleep right through it. It'll be lucky for you if you do, because if they find you inside they'll get in and cut your throat. Where is your car?"

"It's a couple miles down the road, where that guy who fixes cars is."

"It's safe there. But you'll freeze in your car. It gets cold here at night. I'd let you sleep in back, but I have to turn the heat off when we close. Hold on a minute."

He went into a back room. He came back several minutes later, telling me he had phoned a priest who was a friend of his at a monastery in the mountains. "You're in luck. You can stay there tonight. Just follow the road north through Laro and stay on it. It's about three miles. You can't miss the lights of the monastery. Say hello for me. Tell him you're the kid from Iowa."

"Thanks a lot," I said.

"Yeah. Pull the hood of your sweatshirt up when you get to Laro. Walk fast, and don't stop to talk to anyone. Good luck."

Outside it was cold, dark now with a few stars but no moon, silent, only desert on both sides of me. Beyond the feeble light of the windows of the bar, I couldn't see a step ahead. Slowly my eyes adjusted.

In about a mile I reached Laro, a hilly little town of dirt roads and adobe houses clustered together. I kept my hood up, my head down, and walked swiftly. A mongrel sniffed and yapped at my heels, but otherwise the street was empty. I passed a run-down grocery store and a tavern plastered with flaking tin signs, Spanish music wailing on a juke box, and, on the outskirts of town, a convent, the statue of the Virgin looking ghostly in its spotlight.

I knew very little about the Spanish, but I was wary of the young men, even before the bartender's warning. To me they were all hot-blooded and hated Anglos.

The night grew colder and darker as the empty road began climbing through steep banks and shadowy pine. I hurried along, glancing behind me every few feet, not knowing how far I had to walk or what I might encounter in the darkness, afraid of the sound my footsteps were making.

What was ahead, I wondered. In my mind I saw monks in sandals and brown hooded robes, their crowns shaved. I pictured them praying and chanting, pacing up and down long cloistered halls while they read from their missals, and sleeping in their clothes in small cells on straw mattresses.

There was only the silence of the mountain and the blackness ahead. Finally, far ahead on my left I began to see lights and the dark shapes of buildings.

A sign says, "Ring bell and wait for gate master." Beyond the gate are several acres of lawn, scattered cottonwoods and evergreens, a flood-lighted statue of the Virgin, and a long, two-story, flat-roofed building of Spanish-style architecture with a tall wooden cross on its roof. I ring the bell, hear a dog bark and a door slam, and then a man comes across the yard. I am surprised that he is not wearing a monk's habit.

"Hello there!" he calls.

"Hi! My name's Bill. I'm the guy from Iowa."

"I'm Father Bede from Heaven," he grins. "Let's go in and get warm."

The room we enter is large and dimly lit, the high open ceiling crossed with heavy beams. In the middle of the opposite wall is a fireplace big enough for three men to crouch in, and the chimney stones are blackened halfway to the ceiling. On either side of it are tall double doors with glass panes that lead into a grassy, spotlighted courtyard, bordered by a cloistered walk leading to the monks' cells.

We sit on a long deacon's bench in front of a roaring cedar fire. It is very quiet, and I wonder where the monks are. Sleeping probably.

"Are you hungry?" Father Bede asks. He is short and stocky, about forty, very fair in complexion, with a ragged, sandy crewcut. His blue corduroys are faded and worn and his tan cloth coat is greasy and spotted with its cuffs frayed.

I lie that I'm not. Then he asks me where I am headed. I tell him that I have come from Denver; that my car broke down; that I'm on my way to Carlsbad to find work. He asks me how old I am, and I tell him twenty-four. Suddenly it is a great relief to have someone to talk to again.

He scrutinizes me intensely. I am twenty-four, but I know that I look four or five years younger than that. I am fairly tall but slender, thin-faced, with only a few cat whiskers, a thick head of brown hair combed back in a Woody Woodpecker pompadour, with a fair complexion.

"Did you know that we monks are contemplatives?" he asks, glancing at my pants' pockets which are bulging with a pair of clean socks, underwear, T-shirt, safety razor, and toothbrush. "Other orders mingle with the outside world and serve it. But we reject the outer world. We want to be left alone."

I nod.

"Do you know that we take four vows: Poverty, chastity, obedience, and stability?"

"No, I didn't."

"Do you know that when the priest says Mass, he eats and drinks the actual blood and flesh of Christ? Well, Bill," he says, pausing, "it's late, I'll show you to your room. In the morning we'll have plenty of time to talk."

Father Bede picks up some sheets, a blanket, and a pillow, tucks them under his arm and leads me with a flashlight to a crumbling adobe building down in an orchard of dead apple trees, quite isolated from the monastery proper. It is a small room with white walls, the plaster cracked open and the laths exposed, a curtainless window, a rounded fireplace sloping out from one corner of the room, a chair which is wired together, and a cot. A framed color print of Our Lady of Guadalupe and a crucifix hang on the wall.

Father Bede and I make the bed. "This is makeshift, I know, but I hope you'll be comfortable," he says. "The bell will ring at six for Mass. You're welcome to come but you don't have to. Breakfast is at seven. Sleep well. Goodnight."

I have no real idea of where I am or what things look like, just a sense of the remoteness and unearthly stillness of the mountains. There is no sound of traffic, no sound of human activity, no sound even of the wind.

There is no lock on the door. I feel uneasy about the other empty rooms, but I undress and turn out the light. The window is open and the crisp mountain air smells good.

I fall asleep, happy for the clean sheets and quiet, thinking of the words I would use in the morning to thank Father Bede and planning how to make a quick, graceful exit.

"By every consideration possible, withdrawal from the world is beneficial" — *Diadocus, Bishop of Photice in Illyria*

*T*he sun wakes me early and I dress quickly and go outside to see where I am. The statue I saw last night I recognize as Our Lady of Guadalupe, patron saint of New Mexico. An old bus stands in the yard. A big dog, black snoot covered with scar tissue, jumps off an old couch near the entrance to the friary and comes loping over in a business-like manner. I had heard Father Bede call him Big Boy and I call his name. He tears around the yard in wide circles, coming back to me each time, yelping. We start down through the pasture behind the friary.

The monastery lies in a broad, flat valley cut by a river deep and narrow and thickly wooded along its banks. The valley is bordered on the west by foothills dotted with bright patches of red clay and green pine, and on the east, the Guadalupe Mountains.

I am awed by the wildness and immensity of the valley. The air is crisp, the light brilliant and clear, and the sky is immense. In a few minutes the monastery bell gongs from half a mile away and the sound echoes sharp and clear like sound traveling across water.

When I come into the friary, Father Bede is warming himself in front of the fire. He is dressed in a black habit now and I note the hood of a red sweatshirt under his monk's cowl. "Good morning," he says cheerfully. "Are you hungry?"

The bell atop the roof gongs again, making the wooden supports creak and whine like a lonesome puppy, as we go upstairs for breakfast. The refectory is an austere, high-ceilinged room with bare, white walls, very bright in the morning sun. A hand-lettered sign under the wall clock reads *Laborare est orare.*

At each place is a wooden ring with a linen table napkin through it.

There are no introductions and no one pays me the slightest attention, not even a glance. Father Bede motions me to a chair and we stand with our heads bowed. A tall, stout man at the head of the table, the Father Superior, mumbles the blessing while he reaches for the coffee pot and crosses himself as if he were brushing away a fly. Everyone sits down quickly, scraping his chair noisily.

There are seven of us around the table: Two white-collared priests and four brothers, rugged, well-fed and healthy-looking, quite in contrast to the pale ascetics I had expected. All but one of them wear black habits, hoods down, snug-fitting from the shoulders to the waist, and wide leather belts with brass buckles.

It doesn't seem to me that seven monks are very many for such a large monastery. I sense a mystery enveloping their lives.

A big man with tattoos who is not in a monk's habit brings in the food. Women wear aprons, I think to myself; men just roll up their shirt sleeves. I am startled by his cauliflower ears that have shriveled into small buttons, and by his flattened nose.

No one talks, and hand signals are used to ask for food. When you make a fist you get the coffee, and if you make a squeezing motion, the milk is passed. Bread is a horizontal motion with a flat hand, and to get the butter you rub your palms together.

The monk on my left nudges me. He is wearing a T-shirt and has tattoos on each forearm, one reading "U.S. Marines." He is powerfully built, obviously a body builder, with a huge chest, broad shoulders, beautifully developed triceps and biceps.

"Just reach," he whispers. "No one passes food around here unless you ask for it; you could starve first."

Everyone dives in. The homemade corn bread with butter and maple syrup tastes very good. So do the bacon and eggs, a bowl of hot cereal, two glasses of milk, and a cup of coffee that I wolf down.

Father Bede tosses an orange to me the length of the table, startling me. I reach for seconds on the corn bread.

The monk on my left nudges me again and whispers, "Where are you from?"

"Iowa," I reply.

The Father Superior glares at us, but he continues talking in a low voice: "I hitchhiked through your state once. I stopped at a carnival near Keokuk. They had a guy who would take on anybody in wrestling. He'd flex his muscles, taunt the crowd, and offer ten dollars to any man who could stay in the ring with him for three minutes without being pinned.

"I needed the money and I like a challenge. But when I stepped into the ring, I saw that he was twice my size, and it was too late to back out . . ."

"Silence!" the Father Superior snaps, interrupting him. "I want silence."

I turn red, rattling the cup on my saucer, sloshing coffee. There is no talking for the rest of the meal. And there is no dawdling or lingering over second cups of coffee. When the Father Superior has finished eating, he brushes the crumbs off his lap, jerks his chair back, and stands up, a signal apparently for the others, who all join suit. Only ten minutes have elapsed since we sat down, and I still have food on my plate and my mouth is full. There is a murmur of prayer, signs of the cross all around, and we troop out. I follow the monks downstairs to the friary, uneasy about what has happened at the table, and catch up with the one who had sat next to me.

"I was really enjoying your story," I tell him, hoping our conversation hasn't gotten him in trouble. "But how did it end?"

"Oh, we circled and feigned a little," he says, "and then he charged me, using every dirty trick in the book, punching, gouging and head-butting . . ."

"Weren't there any rules?" I ask. He seems pleased at my interest.

"Not in his book. So I got him in an old-fashioned hammer lock, held him down, and he couldn't break it. He finally begged me to let him up: 'Let me up, let me up, we'll call it a draw.' 'Not till the time's up,' I told him. 'I could break your neck.' When the three minutes were up, the timekeeper signalled. I asked for my money. The manager hollered, 'Nope, it wasn't three minutes, you were ten seconds short. I won't pay.' 'To hell he was,' someone yelled. 'Pay up or we'll wreck the tent.' The manager didn't believe him. 'Get your butt out of here or my men will fry it like a slab of bacon,' he threatened me.

"The crowd started tearing the stands apart, board by board, throwing them in the ring. The whole crowd pitched in. The manager wilted like dry lettuce: 'I'll pay, I'll pay.' "

"So you got your money?"

"I treated everyone to beer and ice cream."

"Thanks, that's a good story," I tell him. "But just thinking about Iowa makes me homesick."

Then I see that Father Bede is waiting for me. He motions to me and leads me out of doors. I ask him who the monk I talked to is.

"That's Brother Frank," he says. "He works in the bakery. I hope you're not in a hurry, Bill; I want to show you around."

He shows me the small cinderblock print shop out in the pasture, where one of the monks is employed printing letterheads and advertising brochures for businesses.

The original property was purchased by the Mother Abbey in Michigan, he tells me. "But we are autonomous and completely self-sufficient. We make our own rules, and we get no help or money from the Abbey or from the church. We have to make it on our own, either swim or sink."

He shows me the bakery, where the monks bake bread for the monastery and for outlets in Carlsbad and beyond.

Father Bede is a very intense, vigorous man. He asks if I have any brothers or sisters.

"Two brothers, one a twin."

"What are they doing?"

"They're both students."

"And your father, what line of work is he in?"

"He's dean of a college in Iowa."

"Are you a student, too? What brought you so far from home?"

"I was a student," I reply. "I finished a year of college, though it took three semesters. Did poorly in high school, too, and was held back a year. I struggled halfway through the first semester of my sophomore year but couldn't make it. I lived at home and for a year I had a series of short-lived 'quit this one, quit that one' jobs. The last one was in a factory. Lot of bullies; spit on your shoe when you walk by and pretend it's an accident; throw grease rags at the back of your head. That job was the last straw. Came out here in May, bellhopped at a hotel in Denver, quit this fall, and ended up here in Laro."

"What are your plans?" he asks.

"I don't really know yet." I like Father Bede, but his questions make me uneasy.

"Bill, just tell me to mind my own business if I sound too nosy."

"No, you're not being nosy," I reply.

I would like to tell him, though I can't quite do it, that I'm through with school.

I could have told him that although I come from a family background where education and academic achievement are all-important, I was always the class-room dunce, the gym-class spastic, and the playground punching bag, always dragging behind me a rock skid of Cs, Ds, and Fs.

In the early grades it got to the point where the teacher, having given directions to the class, would add, "Now, Bill, we are going to do this . . .," repeating the instructions for me. Even then I couldn't follow them.

My father tried to tutor me, but it frequently ended up with both of us in tears; my father asking, in desperation, "Goddam, are you stupid, are you dumb, why can't you remember what three times three is after I've told you so many times?" My well-meaning parents, who loved me and were at a loss, would warn me, "Someday you'll be sorry if you don't try harder," which left me, even at an early age, with a terrifying feeling of rejection and defeat.

In the second grade we had a group I.Q. test. The teacher read a dozen questions to us, one by one, with a short period after each for our checks or circles. I could never be hurried. Often I didn't know the answer anyway. Then came the instruction, "Draw a rabbit." Drawing rabbits was something I could do. All of a sudden I was drawing rabbits at a furious pace. I drew them everywhere, and let the rest of the test go.

The next week the city elementary supervisor called and told my mother that the test showed I was retarded. Dad was angry with the supervisor. Subsequent testing by a private psychologist showed my intelligence to be normal.

In the fourth grade, my parents sent me to a private day school. On my first day the teacher asked me what ten minus nine was. I could have told her that I didn't know what the word 'minus' meant, but that was talking back to a teacher. We had used the words 'take away' in my public school. She went down the line, "Ten minus eight, ten minus seven, ten minus six," while the class tittered. "Ten minus two, ten minus one, ten minus zero?" I answered none of them. Panic, humiliation, stupidity, all were there. From that day on I was pegged a dummy.

I struggled through high school with the same learning and emotional problems. The class leaders, including my popular twin, banded together in an elite group, strengthening their own identity and self-esteem. I was shunned. My emotion at being rejected by the group was far greater than my interest would have been had I been accepted.

At the end of my senior year my mother made arrangements for me to go to a famous midwest clinic, where the psychiatrist who handled my case told me, "Pack your bag, say 'Bye mom, bye dad,' cut the apron strings and get on with it."

My first year of college was a miserable experience, while my handsome, extroverted twin, the brother I loved and hated, breezed along, was voted 'the neatest looker in the freshman class' by the senior women, made the Dean's list and the Honor Roll, and was pursued by legions of girls, his friendship sought by all his classmates.

I, by then, had reached a state of inner rage at myself for my failures and defeats. I experienced long bouts of agonizing depression and suicidal impulses.

I had hit a boy during the first semester of my sophomore year and almost injured him permanently.

Dad and I were walking home across campus together. As we were passing a dorm, boys yelled from the windows, "Hey, asshole," "Hey,

Dean's prick," "Hey, Twitch!" Dad was pre-occupied and didn't seem to hear. He had warned me from the start that it might be hard to be on the same campus where he was college dean.

"They mistake your silence and fearfulness for arrogance," Dad had told me. "I know," I had replied, "they think I think my shit smells like roses."

I couldn't sleep that night, the pressure inside was unbearable, and finally about midnight I got out of bed, dressed, went down the hill to the dorm and hid behind a shrub near the entrance. Three boys came out. I thought I recognized them as some of the boys who had taunted me. I jumped out from behind the shrub and walked over to them. "There he is, look at that goddam fem," one of them said. I let my anger explode under his eye and he went down, thrashing around on the ground, yelping and sobbing. I fled. Later there were serious repercussions. The doctor phoned my mother and said the boy might lose an eye. That, I would never forgive myself for.

I dropped out of school and went to work in a factory near home. That was when I almost killed a man.

Carl was a welder, a big man with a look of dissipation and depravity about him, half his teeth rotted out, belly slopped over his belt. He taunted me almost daily. "Hey, Bill," he'd say, "you ain't never had a piece of hair pie in your life, have you? I think you're a swish. Are you a dirty cock sucker? You ain't? You just suck clean ones, right?"

On the day it happened that I almost killed him, I had been assigned as his grunt while he dismantled a steel partition with a cutting torch. It was my silence and passivity that infuriated him. "Pssst, hey, Swish," he began, "I bet I could kick your ass 'n' you wouldn't do a goddam thing, jus' stand there with shit in your pants." He was holding the nozzle of his unlit cutting torch a few feet from my face. "Hey, look at this," he demanded sharply, and as I turned my head I looked right into the blinding flash of light as he squeezed the striker and the torch ignited. I couldn't see for several minutes.

"Why did you look?" he asked, laughing. "Why do you always do what I tell ya? That son-of-a-bitch can blind ya for good, Swish." Then he picked up a fire extinguisher full of water, not foam, pumped the handle up and down and doused me.

Satisfied, he went back to work. He squatted down to do some cutting. There was a rack of odds and ends of steel pipes of different lengths a few feet away from where I was standing. I spotted a short piece. I looked back and forth from Carl's neck to the pipe. In a moment of blinding intensity I reached for it, picked it up and raised it, conscious of the terrible consequences and finality of what I was doing, for him and for me.

I heard a piercing whistle, and let the pipe down slowly. It was Clarence, my foreman. He always whistled for me and I hated it. "Grab some clean grease rags and follow me, I need you."

When the noon whistle blew I walked off the job for good.

After that, I didn't know if I'd ever be able to hold onto a job. But with some money I had saved, I left home, ending up in Denver where I bellhopped.

"Now that I've given you the tour," Father Bede says, "let's go up to the kitchen and have another cup of coffee. Bill, God gives us free will. He doesn't like to interfere. But sometimes He has a special purpose that can't be left to chance. I told you that your coming here is no accident. God has special plans for you, and if you are patient and have faith, in time He will reveal these plans to you."

I listen, startled by his seriousness and intensity.

Father Bede goes on. He says that if faith comes easy to a man, that pleases God, but not as much as it does to win over a criminal, a bum, or an alcoholic; that the farther the distance from God, the greater the desire God has to reach him with His love.

Finally, I ask him if any of the monks come from other walks of life and he says yes. Brother Vincent was a farmer from Nebraska.

Brother Patrick had tended bar in his father's pub in Dublin. Brother Thomas was a printer from Indianapolis, and Brother Frank was a commercial fisherman from Boston, among other trades. "Deaf Don who does the cooking and waits on the table is not a monk," he continues. "He's an ex-professional boxer. These are real men."

He tells me that he himself had begun training for the priesthood when he was seventeen, but had not been ordained until he was forty-two.

I ask him why it took so long.

"Because I fought them all the way."

I ask him what he'd done between times, and he tells me he has done many things, including timber-cruising for a lumber company, and had even been a night club entertainer. "I sang and played the piano. I was popular and I had many friends."

Then he asks me if I have been baptized, and I tell him no. "It would be rough on you if anything happened," he says, and he begins to recite from "The Hound of Heaven":

> I fled Him, down the nights and down the days;
> I fled Him, down the arches of the years;
> I fled Him, down the labyrinthine ways
> Of my own mind: And in the mist of tears . . .

"Bill," Father Bede says finally, "it's not hard to become disillusioned in a world—you've had a glimpse of it—of human meanness and cruelty, a world so interested in material things and so blind and indifferent to the suffering, hurt, and needs of others. But we can't really love others, and have others love us, if we shut ourselves up inside.

"God has special plans for you. Why don't you stay with us a while and see what we're like. There are many jobs to do around here, and I could use your help this very day. Think it over. No one will boss you around or tell you what to do. And you can make this place your home, for as long as you want."

I am touched. "Thank you," I say. At this moment I know I'll stay for at least a few days.

Lying in bed that night, well-fed, relaxed, and clean, I remember my room in the old rooming house in Denver:

The single window, six floors up, over-looking a parking lot, the roofs of cars bespeckled with tree sap and bird excrement; the old pair of woman's rubber boots and the quart jar full of urine that someone had left on the closet shelf; the sink, fleas hopping in it, with separate faucets, one too hot and the other too cold; the door, showing the scars of fifty years of openings and closings; the cold-air register with missing grate through which, flat on my stomach, I once peered down into the room below and saw a sweat-and-urine stained mattress with an old man in his underwear curled up on it asleep, the bed surrounded by bundles of yellowed newspapers on one of which lay a valentine heart with an arrow through it.

Now, I am grateful for the feeling of safety, privacy, and quiet, happy to be rid of rented rooms with people on your left and on your right, above and below you; the blaring of TVs and radios; sirens wailing in the middle of suffocatingly hot nights; the slamming of doors with terrific force; loud voices that shrill endlessly.

I think Father Bede is a man I can trust and talk to.

"And distribution was made to everyone according to his need" — Acts 4:35

The next morning Father Bede glances at my ragtag outfit from a Denver Goodwill and says, "Bill, since you're starting a new life with us, let's find you some new clothes," and he leads me down to the laundry room in the basement of the friary.

Along one wall are several shelves of boxes filled with new socks, T-shirts and underwear, all sizes. I marvel at the idea of having everything you need at your fingertips, never having to shop in stores, getting elbowed in crowds. There is a clothes washer and dryer, and an old barber chair in front of a window overlooking the valley.

At Father Bede's direction I help myself to several sets of underclothes. Along another wall are drawers full of old clothes, shoes, and boots. I pick out a pair of khaki pants, a wool Army shirt, and a pair of knee-length rubber boots covered with innertube patches. To complete my outfit, I put on an old cap punched full of holes.

I change clothes and throw the old ones into the boiler with the door ajar to watch them blaze.

"Now you're burning the past threads of your life," Father Bede jokes.

"How about the two or three Oceanside bums who wore them before I did?" I say, remembering the Denver Goodwill store.

" 'Oceanside'?" Father Bede asks.

"That's an eight-story tenement hotel for bums on Larimer Street."

Leaving the basement, I see a monk sitting under the stairwell, half-hidden, his back braced against the step and his feet propped up against the wall—black habit, a stretch of bare shin, then heavy engineer boots with buckles. He is listening to a Hank Williams country-western tune on a small dime-store record player: "We'll go honk-y tonkin', honk-y tonkin' . . ." He looks up at Father Bede defiantly, as if he expects to be scolded, but Father Bede doesn't say anything. Later I learn he is Brother Thomas, who runs the print shop.

As we are coming up the basement steps, we run into a tall, thin Irishman with a rugby-flattened nose that makes him speak with a nasal brogue. He is wearing a bulky sweater, a patched pair of pants with the fly safety-pinned, and a greasy cowboy hat with a wide floppy brim.

"Ah, I see we 'ave a new recruit fer ta join us woolly bums," he says.

"Woolly bums?" I ask Father Bede, after we have passed him.

Father Bede laughs. "That's ol' Brother Patrick. He's full of malarky, he's got the Irish sense of humor. He used to tend bar in his father's pub in Dublin, but he belongs to us now!"

"I'd like to get to know him."

"Hang around, you will."

I am struck by the contrast between life at the monastery, the kindness and generosity of Father Bede, and the world I have come from.

"We don't like intruders pressed against our gate" —
Father Burkhart

For the first few days I occupy myself by pulling up the tall weeds that grow thick around the barn, because Father Bede says they are a fire hazard, and piling them on the worm garden he has started behind the porter's lodge. The worms are to sell to the trout fishermen who fish in the river.

Time passes quickly. As I'm working on my next job, pulling the nails out of a pile of old lumber behind the carpentry shop and restacking the boards, Big Boy catches and swallows a live mole in a single gulp.

"Work has real meaning around here, because our work praises God," Father Bede tells me. "You are probably used to punching a time clock and working forty hours a week for money to eat, buy clothes, and pay your rent. But *we* don't have to work all the time because we all share the work, and we share what we have. There are no time clocks here. And we don't need cars, fancy furniture, TV sets, or junk like that. We *have* everything we need. And when you do work, do so with the thought in mind that this place is your home, for as long as you want it to be."

I listen with great interest. I know very little about communal living, the hippy communes haven't come along yet; sharing work and profits and living a life of simplicity and self-sufficiency appeal to me.

While I work, I see the brothers in their black habits going back and forth to the bakery, and I wonder what it's really like to reject all material possessions like cars, clothes, and homes, and live for the rest of your life in a small cell with a cot, dresser, and writing table. I like the austerity of their clothing, no bright sportswear, neckties and suits; the austerity of their way of life; the austerity of the monastery itself with its uncarpeted floors, bare walls, curtainless windows, and a few pieces of simple furniture, without knickknacks or figurines on top of the TV set, shag carpets, stiffly-posed unnatural family color portraits taken by a studio photographer—'junk', as Father Bede says. I sense the appropriateness of the spartan monastical life to the austerity of the bleak valley itself.

After I finish the chores around the barn, I rake up a big pile of leaves in the yard. I look up from my work and Brother Frank, who sat next to me at breakfast the first morning, is standing there. "Take it easy, don't kill yourself," he says. "You're doing a fine job. Go ask Deaf Don to give you a cup of coffee."

"What are you going to do with those leaves? Let the wind blow 'em all over hell?" Father Burkhart growls at me, as I enter the friary at lunch time.

It is my first meeting with Father Burkhart, the Father Superior. His rebuff stings.

I had felt elated this morning by the outdoor work, taking pride in what I was doing and how nice things looked. I'd raked up every dead blade of grass, every twig, every leaf.

After lunch, while I am piling the leaves on an old tarp from the barn, the old feeling of never doing things right floods over me. Father Burkhart, I think, with his scowling, harsh manner, has made it clear that I am an unwanted guest at the monastery. Brooding, I wrestle with the thought of throwing down my rake and leaving.

Every job has criticisms and rebuffs and most people weather them. But for me, the slightest criticism reconfirms my own doubts about my worth—or lack of worth, as old Mrs. Wolfe had tried, not so subtly, to demonstrate.

In the spring of my first semester as a college sophomore, having dropped out of school, my father had hired me to clear an acre of black locust from a meadow on a hundred and sixty acres of wooded land he owned in Wisconsin. He and my mother thought that the fresh air and hard physical work might help me with my problems, help me gain some confidence. My father made arrangements through a small country grocery store for me to stay at a house across the road from our woods with a Mrs. Wolfe, the nearest neighbor for miles around in this remote area. I bought a chain saw, threw some clothes in my Chevy, and began the long trek north.

Mrs. Wolfe and I had never met. It was late in the afternoon when I arrived; she was gone, but a note on the door told me to go on in. Just as the sun was setting, she walked like an apparition into the living room, where I was dozing in the dim light. Startled by her appearance, I was speechless. Finally she spoke, icily: "I dint think you was comin', I was expectin' yer father; he woulda been right up my alley." Not misnamed, she was startlingly ugly, jut-jawed with an enormous nose, deep, piercing, furtive eyes, thick, gray, wiry hair brushed straight back and chopped off in a wide shelf at the back of her neck. Her dark, leathery, deeply-lined face had patches of skin cancer from years of exposure to the sun.

She had lived off the land all her life, our land across the road. Fish from the lake, rabbits, frog legs, turtles, mushrooms, hickory nuts, and the squirrels she'd shoot at daybreak from her second-story bedroom window with a .22 were free.

Reclusive and gruff, she barely tolerated my presence. In the evenings in her mink coat for warmth (after her husband's death a few years earlier, she had blown the insurance money on a mink coat and a spree to try to find another man), she would sit silently across the room and stare at me, completely unsettling me, or else prowl restlessly through the cold, dimly-lit rooms. The fur coat made her appear even more wolfish, and her aimless pacing gave me the chills. The incongruity of the beautiful fur and her ugly, wolf-like features was striking.

The only time she would speak to me was to remind me that she was stronger physically, more able, and more of a man than I. I disliked her intensely, but I never let on.

At the supper table one night, she was struggling with the lid on a jar of mushrooms. "May I help you with that, Mrs. Wolfe?" I asked.

"WHAT!" she shrieked, "you think you is stronger than ME? You sure as hell ain't, kid. I ain't afraid to tell ya out loud, you got hands like a girl's and you ain't never gonna get them goddam trees cut down."

I sat there, my hand shaking so hard that I had to put my fork down. Trying to change the subject, I asked her where she found the mushrooms.

"Hee, hee, hee, I ain't gonna tell ya. Found 'em in the woods and that's all you're gonna know."

I excused myself, went to my room, closed the door and brooded, furious at the old lady, and at myself for being so upset but passive.

How could I let an old woman throw me into such inner turmoil? Why was I so easily hurt or threatened by what people said to me? My father had told me frequently, "You're like a wounded rabbit. The minute somebody says something you don't like, you crawl into a hole and stay there. You take things too seriously."

"Dammit," I'd tell him, furious, "do you think I enjoy being the way I am? I don't know why I'm that way; it makes life miserable."

Every morning was the same: "Hey, it's eight o'clock in the morning, ya finally up to stay, kid? I been up since five, I always am. I went ice fishin', caught three panny fish, cleaned 'em 'n' ate 'em, climbed up on the roof ta nail down that goddam shingle the wind blowed loose, then I shoveled out the driveway, foot of snow, to save you the job so ya can get yer car out; then I hiked two miles to the grocery store, six below, so ya could

34

have yer shitty frozen Toast'ems cause you won't eat fresh fish for breakfast, and you is still in bed sleepin'. Kids today is sure soft. But then I don't expect no one ta keep up with me."

I loved my father's woods with the same intensity that I disliked the old woman. Hidden in a dense forest of tall pines was a granite boulder as big as a garage, accessible by shinnying up a birch. It was flat on top and held the sun's warmth, a perfect spot to eat lunch or to sit and think. I was going to build a house on it some day.

One night I decided to go fox hunting and, lonely, I asked her if she wanted to go with me.

I wore a lamp attached to a headband, the beam tilted upwards to pick up the glow of the eyes of the fox as he approached. Our shotguns loaded, a bucket of fresh cow manure nearby to cover our scent, we lay on our stomachs in an open field in an Indian burial ground, under the bright stars and a full moon, deep in the silence and stillness of my father's woods. The only sounds were the shrill squeal of the rabbit call I was blowing to imitate a rabbit in distress and the eerie, faraway baying of farmers' dogs.

"Well, kid, you sure was up late tonight, 'n' we dint see a single damn fox. I 'magine ya'll have ta sleep till noon tomorrow."

One morning I sawed down by mistake, and into firewood lengths, a black walnut tree worth several hundred dollars.

"Woosh, kid, don't ya even know the difference 'tween a goddam black locust 'n' a black walnut?" Mrs. Wolfe sneered. "I'd a told ya if ya asked me."

Two days later, she fell twelve feet out of a big hickory tree while gathering nuts and broke her hip. She wasn't as tough as she thought she was. The ambulance took her to the hospital. I packed my bag and drove back home, discouraged, my work unfinished.

It was then that I embarked on a year of short-lived jobs, culminating in the factory job where I met Carl the welder who launched my trip to Denver.

I look up suddenly and see Father Bede standing there. I'm so startled I drop the rake.

"Bill, I want to talk with you," he says in a serious tone of voice. "Father Burkhart was away on business the night you arrived here and I was in charge. I let you spend the night here. The next day I invited you to stay on with us . . ."

My hopes plummet. Father Bede appears shaken.

"But Father Burkhart is in charge now. He's my superior. I want you to go and talk to him. Tell him a little bit about yourself. Tell him why you want to stay here. Just be relaxed and be yourself. Now would be a good time; he's in his cell."

Feeling deep apprehension, I walk through the friary and into the courtyard to the door of Father Burkhart's cell, not knowing yet exactly what I'm going to say, dreading what the outcome might be.

I knock.

"Yah, come in," Father Burkhart shouts.

He is sitting at a desk strewn with papers in his small cell. "Sit down," he says impatiently, "I've only got a minute or two. What do you want?"

"Father Burkhart," I say, "if I could stay around here a while, I'd make myself as useful as I can. I'm handy, I can do a lot of things, paint, wash windows, anything. I'd stay out of the way, I'd work hard . . ."

"Hold on a minute, listen to me. We're a religious order. We're contemplatives, we're monks. We don't *like* visitors, they distract us. We can't take in every stray who presses a runny nose against the gate, and we're not running a boarding house or a hotel. Father Bede thinks you're a lost sheep. We don't have facilities for sheep either. You have a home in Iowa, he says. Why don't you go home? Well, I'm not going to tell you to stay, I'm not going to tell you to leave. Father Bede made a good case. He got down on his hands and knees to plead for you. It's against my better judgment, but let's see how useful you can make yourself. We'll play it by ear, *my* ear."

"Thank you, Father Burkhart," I say, tremendously relieved. "I'll work hard, I really will, and I promise not to do anything to make you regret it."

Father Bede is out in the yard waiting for me, and I tell him what Father Burkhart said.

"Hey, that's great, buddy," he says, clapping me on the back. "Father Burkhart has never before allowed any visitors from outside to stay here. Bill, things will work out. Have patience. And remember, I need you and trust you and have faith in you."

Later that afternoon Father Bede and I go for a walk in the valley along the river.

"Is Father Burkhart always so gruff?" I ask as we walk. "He bawled me out for leaving a pile of leaves."

"Don't let it upset you," Father Bede says. "Sometimes Father gets a little hot under the clerical collar."

Then I tell him how Brother Frank, the one with tattoos on his arms who works in the bakery, came up while I was working and told me to take it easy. "Kind of him, wasn't it."

"That's Brother Frank. He's drifted and knocked around a lot, even stepped outside the law, and knows something about the underworld. He has brains to match his muscles. He has his problems, too, but I'm trying to help him. It won't be easy. I pray for him. I hope you two will get acquainted. He can help you, and perhaps you can help him."

I have no way of knowing now that we, Brother Frank and I, will become close friends, or of the sorrow he will bring to the monastery and the upheaval it will cause in our lives.

About half a mile south of the monastery, the vast open fields of tall dry grass end, and we enter a dense forest.

"Isn't this beautiful," Father Bede exclaims, swinging his arms wide. "Eleven hundred acres of it belong to the monastery. The

Indians from the pueblo here in Laro hunted and fished here until a hundred and fifty years ago, and it isn't any less wild today than it was back then. We'll do lots of exploring around here, you and I. We'll hike back in the mountains and I'll show you some Indian signs I discovered on a rock ledge, black hand prints made with pigment from animal bile that are a real find."

"My first morning here, Father Bede, I hiked down in the pasture with Big Boy and I had such a longing to explore. I didn't know then that I'd ever have a chance."

"You will now. And there's a Spanish boy, Ernie, a great kid, who works in the bakery. His uncle was hiking back in some remote canyon in the mountains and stumbled upon pueblo ruins. Ernie told me his uncle is the only one who knows its whereabouts, that judging from the artifacts still lying around he was probably the first visitor since the pueblo was abandoned perhaps a hundred or more years ago. He has a four-wheel-drive jeep and he's offered to take Ernie and me back there. You'll come with us. We'll arrange it soon, before the first snowfall."

"I can't wait to see that. I know so little about this part of the country but it fascinates me."

We sit down to rest in an area of fallen timber. "We should clean this place up," Father Bede says. "The Boy Scouts could use it; we let them camp around here. The trout fishermen could use it, too. There'd be plenty of firewood."

"I have a chain saw at home," I say. "I could have it shipped to me on the bus."

"You could? Fantastic, buddy. And later we'll set up stations of the cross. But first I'd better check with Father Burkhart. Well, let's head back."

An hour later he tells me, "Father Burkhart thinks it's just some fly-by-night scheme that will never be completed. But he said okay, so let's show him what we can do."

"That's great. I'll write home for my saw this evening. I'll show Father Burkhart how handy I am with that chain saw; I cut both knees out of my coveralls learning how to use it."

Laughing, Father Bede says, "We have better ways around here to wear out your knees and get a good hookup with aerospace at the same time."

"Aerospace?"

"God."

Extreme mistrust of others can become a disease

Though I am beginning to enjoy my new life, I am aware that I am a guest, an outsider, even an intruder, and I have always hated to impose on anyone. To most of the brothers, I know that I am only a face that comes to meals with Father Bede, and it's all right with me to keep it that way. But before long, faces begin to merge with names and personalities, and I develop some sense of their daily activities.

Work is interspersed throughout the day with the canonical hours of prayer and devotion. The chapel bell gongs me awake each morning at five, while it is still dark, for Matins, then Mass. It rings for Sext before lunch; None, after lunch; Vespers, before supper; and for Complin, the last prayer service of the day, at nine each evening. It echoes through the valley and the sound seems close, yet far off. I can hear the agonized whine and creak of the bell's wooden supports atop the friary; it's a sad sound.

After breakfast Father Burkhart lumbers off to his cell to his correspondence and bookkeeping.

Brother Thomas, a lanky, big-boned, twenty-six year old printer, strides off to his print shop down in the pasture. "He's run the monastery into a $10,000 debt with that little newspaper he prints," Father Bede tells me, "and he even rakes the monastery over the coals in it. When I was in charge, while Father Burkhart was away, he'd leave the print shop and run off into town every chance he got. He's a young, healthy, good-looking kid, and I knew that wasn't right. I put a stop to it. He and Father Burkhart are actual brothers. When Father came back, I was sitting in his cell and Brother Thomas came bursting in, shouting 'Get that guy out of here!' "

Brothers Frank, Patrick, and Vincent troop off to the monastery bakery: Frank, in his early forties, the commercial fisherman; Patrick, about the same age, the bartender from Dublin; Vincent, a dark, husky farm boy in his early thirties. Brother Vincent mixes the dough, gives the orders, and keeps the books.

If you need to have a button sewed on or a sock darned, Father Alphonse will do it. If you need an aspirin or a bandage, you go to Brother Thomas who is in charge of first-aid. Brother Vincent cuts hair. If you run out of toilet paper or soap, you go to Brother Patrick, who also takes care of changing the bedsheets and emptying the wastepaper baskets. If you need to be tucked in at night, you are out of luck.

I volunteer for my first task of each day by writing on a sheet of note pad in the kitchen, "Don, may I wash dishes for you?"

Deaf Don, an ex-professional boxer who lost his hearing in the ring, is a big, jolly, energetic man in his early fifties.

"He fought his last professional fight when he was thirty-seven," Father Bede had told me. "He knocked the guy out with one punch, flatter than a penitent at the Pope's feet, after the bell had rung, because he couldn't hear it. That's when he had to quit boxing."

Deaf Don is dietician, cook, waiter, bus boy, and dish washer. His kitchen, adjoining the refectory, is clean and bright. He works alone in the kitchen all day with no one for company.

But after the dishes are washed, we always talk. If I say one word at a time and exaggerate the sound of it, he can read my lips by repeating each word back to me, grunting and stammering in a loud voice until he gets the right sound.

He always has a loud, friendly greeting for me whenever I walk into the kitchen: "Lef-ty Lou! Lef-ty Lou!" he shouts, bobbing and weaving about, throwing wild, imaginary punches at me.

To speed up the conversation, we write things down. When I ask him where he is from, he writes, "From a lot of places." He writes that he is happy at the monastery and wants to stay here the rest of his life. He wants to be buried near the chapel in an open grave, no coffin, with a simple wooden cross for a marker, the way monks are.

After I finish helping Deaf Don with the breakfast dishes, Father Bede and I may sit on the deacon's bench in the friary and talk about his plans for me for that day.

"I don't know what you two find to talk about," he says. "But you've sure made a friend in Deaf Don."

"It must get lonely when you can't hear the sound of another human voice."

"It's so hard to converse with him, Bill, that none of us really takes the time we should, but we love him.

"Well, Bill, let's kick 'er in the gas. We're just bone 'n' gristle, you 'n' I, but God will chew us up and spit us in the Devil's eye."

Already I can see many aspects of monastic life that are profoundly worthwhile. But to live a life of chastity would, it seems to me, be a great sacrifice.

I have never had a real girl friend. I'm afraid of girls, especially the attractive ones, even more so if they show an interest in me, which some do, and I freeze in their presence. The greater the desire, the more miserable I feel.

In Denver, bellhopping at the hotel, one of my jobs had been to fill the lobby Coke machine, for which I had a key. And in the back of the machine at her request, I stored a quart of milk for Cheryl, thirty, a prostitute who had a room on the third floor. Cheryl, with her natural, flaming red hair, thick and bouncy, her pale white skin, and compact figure, was startlingly beautiful. She suffered from a stomach ulcer and I took her a glass of milk every evening. Always appreciative in a touching, apologetic way, as if no one had ever done her a favor, she would ask me to sit down and talk a while as she sipped her milk gingerly, wincing each time she swallowed. She had had her esophagus removed, she said, and it hurt as the cool liquid fell directly into her stomach.

Cheryl stayed in her room all day, only going out at night. I never saw her in the dining room, sitting around the lobby, in the bar, or chatting with Ed, the desk clerk. I sensed her isolation and alienation.

I was always nervous with Cheryl, six years older than I, over-whelmed by her beauty and sexual attractiveness.

During the day Cheryl looked as fresh-faced and wholesome as a farm girl. At night when she went out, hidden under a giant blond wig, behind layers of make-up, in a gaudy miniskirt, the transition always shocked me. One evening, when I brought her her milk, she was standing in front of a mirror applying a brown liquid to her neck and shoulders, then, reaching under her off-the-shoulder dress, she rubbed it on her breasts, fully exposing them, while I stood there riveted. "This is Man-Tan. I have to use it. Sorry, Bill," she said apologetically.

Cheryl accumulated men's jewelry, tarnished, not new, wrist watches, rings, tie clasps, cuff links, and on my day off I'd drive her to a pawn shop on Larimer Street to hock her trinkets. One morning we made a special trip across town, Cheryl still in her blond wig, make-up, gold satiny miniskirt and matching pumps, seated next to me on the ragged upholstery of my old car, to pawn her booty of the night, a bowling ball.

Cheryl had to return to the hospital for further surgery. At the end of the week I bought her a pack of cigarettes, took along an envelope Mr. Singer, our boss, had given me, and went to see her. She was so grateful she cried. "No one else gives a damn," she said. I gave her the envelope, but it wasn't a get-well card. She had been sleeping with Mr. Singer in exchange for her room and it was a bill for the week of her absence. "That son-of-a-bitch," Cheryl said in tears. She held my hand and told me she had an infection in her abdomen and the doctors were looking for it but they couldn't find it.

"Do your mother and father know you're in the hospital?" I asked.

"No, they don't. They don't know where I am, and I don't want 'em to. I'm splitting when I get out of here."

"Where will you go? You'll be missed."

"I don't know yet. But somewhere."

I had a hard time asking her what I wanted to, but finally I got my courage up: "How would you like to come back to Iowa with me?"

"Do you mean that, Bill? Yes, I'd like to."

Ten days later Cheryl went off to Las Vegas with a man she met in the hotel bar who told her he'd make her a show girl.

Shortly after that I quit my job at the hotel and headed for the southwest.

Dreamed-for solitude: An escape from the gnashing, grinding, and abrasion of daily life

I write home for my chain saw. Then I wait for it to come. It seems to take forever. Finally, one noon, as I sit down at my place for lunch, my knees bump something under the table—a large box. My saw is inside. After lunch Father Bede tells me it had arrived at Alejandro's on the bus this morning and Father Burkhart drove in to get it. It was his idea to hide it under the table.

For the next week I start out early every morning with the saw on my shoulder, along with a ten-cent tin cup for measuring oil, a red-handled screw driver, and three rat-tail files. Big Boy always tags along. I am fairly good with the saw. I can adjust the carburetor settings while the saw is cutting, and I can notch the tree on the opposite side and line up the cut so that the tree falls right where I want it, neat and clean without splitting. I like the whine of the saw, the clouds of oily smoke, the shower of sawdust, the smell of the wood, and the hard physical work. I like the dime tin cup and the red-handled screw driver and the rat-tail files. But most of all I like the bleakness, wildness, and stillness of the valley, and at moments I feel an overwhelming sense of longing and beauty.

I enjoy being by myself, working for fun instead of pay, and most of all I enjoy the freedom from bosses.

It is good at the end of the day to come back tired, to food and rest and the company of others.

Although I have to sit back in the dimly-lit pews by myself I always go to Complin. I enjoy the stillness and solemnity, the monks gliding silently like shadows into the chapel from the vestry, their faces hidden inside their black hoods. They kneel in their choir stalls and then the chanting begins. The other voices blend well but Father Bede's clear tenor is the best.

I try to figure out which voice belongs to which habit, but I can always identify big Father Burkhart. He crouches on one knee, easier to get back up, I suppose, or perhaps he is afraid that if he leans too hard on the rail, it may come crashing down. He looms head and shoulders above the others and leads the chanting in the deep, gruff voice of a factory foreman shouting orders.

Prayer ends with the Office of the Dead. Then the monks genuflect, cross themselves, and file out silently through the vestry to their cells in the courtyard, the last one turning off the lights and closing the door behind him.

I sit there until I hear the last cell door close, and then all is silent and dark.

If anyone turns on his light after Complin, he has to have a good reason and be able to explain it to Father Burkhart. "Why were you burning your light last night?" he snaps at me. I tell him I'd been reading in bed. "We don't waste electricity around here. Don't let me catch you doing it again."

It is a city-block's distance from the chapel to my room in the old building down in the apple orchard. I have to shuffle along flat-footed in the darkness, arms outstretched, and it is then, my skin prickling, that I recall a discussion I had with Father Bede about the Devil. "I don't believe in him," I had said. "Ah, when you don't believe in him, that's just the time when he's around," Father Bede replied.

Finally, I find the creaky door of my building, and with my ears alert and my eyes watering, feel my way along the wall, past the doors of the other empty rooms, to mine at the end of the hall. And still preserving the mood of quiet, I open and close the door softly, tip-toe to my toothbrush, wash and undress in the dark, careful not to clunk my shoes on the floor. Big Boy always follows me to the front door and sometimes comes in and spends the night on the floor next to my bed. I listen to his even breathing as I fall asleep. We have taken a liking to each other. Brother Vincent found Big Boy at the dog pound: "The monastery needed a watch dog," he says. "I took one look at him, he almost took my arm off. I knew he was the dog for us. He's no house pet!"

At first it is a strange feeling to be so completely cut off from the world, no magazines or newspapers (just war, murders, and horror, Father Bede says), no radio or television, but I don't really miss them. Gradually the solitude and privacy seep into ones blood, so do the howling autumn wind, the hissing radiators in the friary, logs blazing in the fireplace, and the vastness of the mountains and the valley.

"Blessed is he that considereth the poor" — *Psalm 41:1*

One morning Father Bede suggests we drive into Laro with a load of toys and old clothes from the barn.

"We'll give this stuff to some needy families," he says.

I am eager to go because I want to see what the town of Laro is really like and to meet some Spanish people and see how they live. The adobe houses appeal to me—their simplicity, their thick walls, and the protruding pine logs that hold up the ceiling.

"I like this," I say, admiring a black leather coat with heavy lining and corduroy collar and cuffs that I find as we are loading the clothes into the car.

"You already *have* a coat, Bill. We'll scare up another one sometime."

I glance at Father Bede's scruffy coat and am embarrassed by what I said.

Father Bede slides behind the wheel of my car. "I'll drive, Bill. You're likely to drag the anchor."

We rattle over the cattleguard, through the monastery gates, and barrel along down the middle of the narrow, winding mountain road, my feet braking hard against the floorboard, Father Bede pounding the steering wheel with his fist as he sings at the top of his voice: "Oh you can't get to heaven in this old Chev-ee, Bill's old Chev-ee, Bill's old . . ."

When we get to Laro, we climb the winding dirt road to the top of the hill. Father Bede kicks the brakes and we buck to a stop at a small adobe house. "Hello, hello, hello!" Father yells, springing out of the car. A Spanish woman with heavy calves and stringy, knotted hair appears in the doorway as a dozen arms, legs, and faces try to squeeze around her. There are even more children inside. "Hey, Roberto!" Father shouts, patting a small head. "Patricio, how's my boy?" he asks, grabbing another one by the ears.

The room we enter is dark and cheerless, dirt-floored, with yellowed lace curtains, faded wallpaper with a dizzying flower pattern, and old photographs of young men in military uniform hang in a row on the wall in heavy, scrolled wooden frames.

We carry the boxes in and set them on the table. There is much squealing, jumping, and reaching as, with a flourish, Father Bede lifts each item out of the box like a magician pulling a rabbit out of a hat. "Hey, hey, what's this!" he exclaims, holding high a panda, and "Oh my, take a look at this!" A boy about six runs happily to a corner with a dozen shoes all knotted together by the laces. A fair-skinned girl with curly red hair, an Anglo, clutches two pieces of tarnished silverware to her breast and beams. A small hand jerks a bumblebee pull-toy rapidly across the floor. An old Army fatigue hat slips down over the eyes and nose of the little girl who grabs for it. Another child hobbles around gleefully with his foot wedged in a saucepan Father Bede has given him.

"Take this trash out and throw it in the incinerator," Father Bede says, startling me, shoving at me a handful of cheap paperback books.

Suddenly a pair of arms are thrown around my waist, and a voice belonging to the little girl with pale skin and curly red hair calls out something in Spanish.

"She says she loves you," the mother explains, beaming.

Hugging the little girl I tell her, "I love you, too."

In the next room a baby wails. A boy holds a pacifier in the baby's mouth, looks up and grins proudly through the door at us. "He has fits," the mother explains. "We got to watch him so he don't swallow his tongue."

While the other children dance around us, lively and spirited, another fair-skinned child, a boy about eight, standing in a far corner of the room motionless and mute, watches us warily. Stocky, with round cheeks, a big jaw, pug nose, tufts of straw hair sticking out all over the top of his head, he would look pugnacious if it weren't for the bewildered, frightened look on his face. I can't take my eyes off him. I want to approach him, reach out to him in some way, but he catches my eye and darts into the next room.

I ask the woman who he is.

"That's Earlito," she says. "He's real scared of people; something bad must have happened to him. He's from Welfare. He comes from a broken-down family."

"He's very withdrawn," Father Bede adds. "His father is an alcoholic and his brother is in a reformatory. He was living with his eighty-five-year-old grandmother. All they had was each others' company. The boy wasn't even in school. He and granny would spend the entire day rocking in front of the TV."

"What a sad situation that was," I say. "He's got a happy home, here. I hope being with these children will make him less afraid."

"I hope so, too. That's why he's here, Bill."

"The children want you to have some cake," the woman says. "They baked it this morning."

The cake is deep green. The children must have used a whole

bottle of vegetable dye. When I bite into my piece, I almost break a tooth. It is chock full of uncooked elbow macaroni.

"I let them do whatever they wanted," she says proudly.

"I can't believe it, eleven children and another one on the way," I tell Father Bede after we are in the car.

"She's not pregnant, Bill," he says, laughing, clasping his hands over his stomach. "Spanish women don't wear girdles."

"Where did that little red-headed girl with the milky skin come from—Welfare?" I want to talk about Earlito, his face still haunts me, but I can't.

"I don't know. Half of those children are probably her own, and the rest she's just collected. I try to help her the way we did today. I asked her to iron our altar linen, because it would offend her dignity if I didn't ask for something in return. These people don't want charity."

"They're very poor, aren't they?"

"They have very little. There's no industry around here, and you can't farm in the desert. There's not much for them to do. Most of the men have broken-down pickups, and they cut and haul a little firewood. They raise some beans and squash and a few chickens, and most of them gamble on the side."

"Those children love you."

"Bill, I'd like you to get to know them the way I do. I want you to meet some of these families. Once they get to know you, they'll show you so much love you won't believe it. The Spanish are very loyal. They don't take friendship for granted. I have so much feeling for them that I can hardly contain it. It almost does me in."

Next we go to check on the progress of a Laro boy to whom Father Bede has given some wood-carving tools.

"I asked him to carve me a crucifix," Father Bede says. "If he gets good at it, I have some friends who will buy them. He gets into trouble and doesn't seem to have much of a future. I want to help him if I can."

The young man is dark, stumpy, all shoulders, neck and torso,

51

so big around and barrel-chested his arms stick out woodenly. He lives in a dirt-floored, two-room adobe house with his father and step-mother. He is reticent, and Father Bede has to coax him to show us the crucifix.

"It's no good. I don't think you'll like it."

"Won't *like* it, how do you *know* I won't like it? I haven't even seen it. Come on, Tony, my boy, let's see it."

The Christo is very thin and carved from white pine. The tiny hands with thumbs and fingers are attached to the stick arms with a small bit of white cement, and these in turn are fastened to the shoulders with straight pins. A fragile piece of carving has come from hands the size of oak burls.

Deliberate or not, the eyes of Christ seem to have scar tissue around them just like the hard, brutal eyes that he, Tony, has. I'm afraid of him.

"Tony, this is amazing," Father says, admiring it intently. "You have a real gift. Work hard, develop it, and share the fantastic things you make with others."

"It's beautiful," I say.

Father Bede buys it. "I want you to carve me another one, Tony, just like it."

"I don't want to carve anymore, Father," he says.

"These boys don't have much incentive," Father Bede tells me in a discouraged tone of voice when we are back in the car. "You give them something to do and offer to pay them for their work, but they don't seem to care. They'd rather sit on the steps, drink beer and play the guitar. Anyway, it doesn't matter. His father is going to send him away. His new wife is as young as Tony, and he's afraid to have him around.

"A lot of the Spanish really dislike Anglos, don't they?" I say, as we drive back from Laro.

"They're desperately poor. They've been cheated and taken

advantage of. Most of the good farm and ranch land here is in the hands of wealthy Anglos."

"The bartender at Alejandro's warned me that it wouldn't be safe for me to hitchhike or even walk. He said there are gangs of Spanish boys around here."

"You're safe at the monastery, but you wouldn't be safe walking around town. Life is harsh here, Bill. The young boys get booted out of the house as soon as they can tie their own shoelaces and wipe their own butts, because their families can't afford to feed them. They have to fend for themselves to survive and they grow up tough. There *are* gangs. Fights and brawls are very common, and many arguments between the men are settled with a gun or a knife. The boys learn it from their fathers. When I came here, I would worry when I said Mass in Laro. But some of the toughest boys are my friends now, and, if anything started, I know they'd jump to my rescue."

"Look!" he exclaims, slowing, as we are rounding a curve farther down the road. He points out a rectangular hole in the side of a steep clay bank, a few feet below the surface of the bank.

"When they widened the road here, they dug up a guy buried in there with a bullet hole in the back of his head. You can still see the outline of the grave. It had been a fairly recent burial. But there was no investigation. No one even raised an eyebrow. There's no real law around here."

"Some of the Spanish are very attractive, aren't they?" I say. "I like their high cheek bones and dark skin. Many of the women are strikingly beautiful."

Father Bede laughs. "I knew you'd notice the women. Yes, they are when they're young, but they go to seed in a hurry because life is so hard. But the Spanish *are* extremely attractive people.

"Bill, one of our reasons for being here is to serve these people. There is so much suffering and hardship here. I want to help them, but *they* want to let them alone. *They* don't want to have anything to do with these people."

"By 'they', do you mean the monastery?" I ask. Father Bede nods. It makes me feel good that Father Bede confides in me.

"This old Chevy of yours is a gift from heaven, Bill. I don't know what we'd do without it."

"Whose old bus is that squatting in the yard?" I say. "Where did it come from?" It is a brown, diesel Greylines Tour Bus. Its seats are full of broken glass, the aisle from the driver's seat to the rear of the bus is a tangle of ropes, musty tarps, and camping equipment. It was ironic that the license plates read JCB-1075; "Jesus Christ's Bus," I thought to myself.

He tells me that he took the train at Lincoln to go to see his spiritual advisor in Arlington, Texas. It was there that he spotted the bus that had been battered by a hurricane, and drove it back to Laro to use to take the Spanish boys and girls on camping trips.

Father Burkhart was angry when he saw it standing in the yard, and he ordered Father Bede to get rid of it.

"When I can get it running again," Father Bede says, "I may have to drive it into Carlsbad, sell tickets and chance it off. But I'm hoping Father Burkhart will change his mind and let me keep it."

I ask him what's wrong with it.

"It needs a new battery, for starters. And some other repairs. Brother Frank was a mechanic in his father's garage, and I'm counting on him to help me. We have Saturday afternoons free."

"I'm not much of a mechanic, but I'd like to help. I can imagine what a camping trip in that old bus would mean to some of those boys and girls. It's a great idea."

"It's a real comfort to have you around, Bill. You have a real feeling for the Spanish families we visited. And you're always so willing to help. I like that and I think Father Burkhart will see it, too.

"I don't imagine you've ever seen this kind of poverty before. Tell me a little about your home in Iowa."

"It's a dinky little town in the east Iowa hills. The barber is also the mayor. The popular meeting place is Barretts; they've got a barbershop, pool table, and lunch counter all in the same large room. The place is so filthy it would choke a roach. They have an awful slogan: 'Come In To Get Clipped, Whipped, And To Sip.' 'Gossip and Home-Wrecking Parlor,' the locals call it.

"We live on the brow of the highest hill . . ." Suddenly I can't continue, choking on the words.

Father Bede asks what's wrong.

I shake my head. How can I tell him how painful it was for me to leave home. How homesick I am.

"I may bawl," I tell him.

"I'm sorry this is painful for you to talk about, Bill. Sometimes it's good to get these things off your chest. You keep your distance. You don't want others to find out about you. You seem to keep things inside."

Getting my composure back, I continue. "We live in a large, airy, old, high-ceilinged, Grant Wood house with a wide veranda all the way around the front and side, high on a hill. It's on the campus, beautiful and hilly, where my father is Dean. From the window of my room I can look out over miles of plowed fields all the way to the western horizon.

"You're right, there wasn't much poverty where I grew up. Especially the kind of poverty these poor Spanish families endure. But some of the lost, sick, lonely old men I ran into in Denver in that rooming house haven't had easy lives.

"And that hotel where I was a bellhop had its share of indigents. There was a stooped-over old guy waiting at the desk one morning. I picked up his key, grabbed his old suitcase tied together with string and rope, and led him to the elevator. He shuffled after me muttering and sputtering, a querulous old fellow, tottering and feeble, out of the elevator and down the hallway to his room. He was toothless and I couldn't understand a word he said.

"I opened the door and was startled to see that the bed was unmade, and there were soiled towels on the bathroom floor.

"Then the phone rang. It was Ruth, the desk clerk, shrieking, 'What did you do with old Mr. Nagle?'

"I said, 'I just took him up to his room. And it isn't even made up.'

" 'He's a check-out!' she exclaimed. 'His bus is here!'

" 'His bus?' I asked.

" 'The county bus! To take him to the poor farm.' "

Father Bede laughs. "It was clever to try and fi-NAGLE another day's rent out of the old guy."

"That's good, Father. Actually, I goof up so often. I just don't get things straight even though I concentrate. It's happened in school, over and over, and it always happens in jobs."

"Maybe you try too hard. Maybe you get too tense."

"I'm very tense, I know. But I always try to do a good job. I'm conscientious. I work hard."

"You and Brother Patrick, with your tales, are cut from the same cloth. And you both came to us by a circuitous route; Brother Patrick was driving across country, and if it hadn't been for a depraved hitchhiker, he wouldn't have come to us. Ask him about it sometime. And you came to us, one could say, because of *your* bad experiences at the hotel; if it hadn't been for those, you might still be there. Some good often comes out of bad. 'Gather with the vultures,' Sacred Scripture says."

"I had an experience like Brother Patrick's when I started out on my trip, only it wasn't a hitchhiker. I left home that morning and about seventy miles later, feeling homesick already, trying to decide whether to turn around or keep going, I pulled off into a deserted rest stop and fell asleep in the front seat. I was awakened suddenly when I heard the rear car door open. I sat bolt upright as a pair of beefy hands reached over the seat, the hands of a huge truck driver, and started to massage my neck and shoulders. I jerked away, and he said, leering at me, 'I'll bet you're wide awake now, aren't you? Did you like what I was doing?'

"I said, 'No.' I was terrified. Then he said, 'Haven't you ever had any strange stuff?' I didn't know what he meant for a minute. I said, 'No, I haven't, and I don't want any.' He got angry, swore, and said, 'It's just like doing it with a woman, you can't tell the difference.' "

This is the kind of thing I would never have told anyone before, but Father Bede's gentle admonition to me earlier that one shouldn't keep things inside, reassures me.

"I told him, 'Get out of my car, I have to get going.' He was ruffling my hair and trying to stick his hand down the front of my shirt, grabbing my head and rubbing his whiskers on the side of my face.

"I jumped out of the car. He said, 'Don't do that. Drive me up to my rig.' It was a cattle truck parked about three hundred feet from where we were. The rest stop was otherwise deserted. So I got in and drove, with him looming over me in the back seat, anticipating his coming crashing down on me from behind. He got out, uncurling his huge frame, slammed the door violently, and I drove off in a hurry."

"The Devil wears many disguises, Bill," Father Bede tells me. "You were lucky. Thank you for trusting me enough to tell me about some of your experiences."

It is late afternoon by the time we get back to the monastery. After dinner that evening, when I go to my room, I find the black leather coat, the coat I had admired that morning, with the corduroy cuffs and collar, neatly folded on my bed. I put it on to see if it fits and a note drops out: "Father Alphonse will sew on the buttons that are missing."

What shows on the surface seldom indicates what has made that person the way he is

The next morning after breakfast I go straight to Father Alfonse.

Father Alfonse is a fat, bald, timid, preoccupied little French Canadian in his fifties, as shy as a mountain marmot.

In charge of the washing, mending, and ironing, he works alone in the laundry room in the basement of the friary, where there are always two inches of soapy water on the floor.

"We order soap around here by the boxcar load," I heard Father Burkhart complain, "and it'll break us yet. What's a little dirt?"

But Father Alfonse safety-pins his pants' cuffs mid-shin to keep them dry and shovels in the Tide.

The vow of poverty doesn't permit personal possessions, but Father Alfonse, for reasons known only to himself and Father Burkhart, is permitted to own a flashlight. It is next to his plate at meals, and always within arm's reach when he does the washing and ironing.

He is too shy to participate with the others in the reading of the Divine Offices. Instead, he reads them in private with Father Burkhart. He sits at the table with his head bowed and doesn't raise his eyes, even when he signals for food. He never comes to the friary to sit on the deacon's bench in front of the fire.

The instant his work is done, Father Alfonse puts on his habit, goes to the courtyard and begins his pacing. A young monastery cat he calls Britches scampers along at his heels. When she gets underfoot or rolls in his path, Father Alfonse removes the flyswatter stuck in the belt of his habit and swats her gently on the rear. Then he resumes his pacing, up and down, back and forth, hour after hour, mumbling to himself as he reads from his missal, open in one hand, the fingers of the other hand plucking the air, a harp perhaps, and music only he can hear.

"Father Alfonse," I say, "Father Bede gave this coat to me, and I'm really pleased with it. It's warm, too. I wonder, would you mind sewing on a button or two? There's no hurry. I'd be willing to fold sheets and towels for you."

Father Alfonse takes my coat without a word or nod of his head, and gets out needle and thread.

I feel drawn to Father Alfonse.

I remember the summer, having graduated from high school after five years and being near the bottom of the class, that I clerked in my uncle's drug store in the small farm town of Kalona, Iowa.

All summer long I endured almost daily lectures on shyness given by my aunt, a brisk, bubbly, loquacious little woman:

"Oh, my, you're so shy, you make others feel uncomfortable, you surely do, it will turn customers away, my, yes, a sparkling personality is just as important as good grooming, don't you think, and that correspondence school I got my window-display course from has a course in conversation, it's just what you need. I was just like you, I was indeed, until I

went to teachers' college for a semester and lived in a dormitory full of girls, you can imagine how they talk, and I grew up in a hurry, I surely did. You're so timid, Bill, but I know what you need, I know just what you need, a help-mate, yes, indeed, the kind of girl you'll want to settle down and raise a family with, oh, my, yes, and 'they lived happily ever after' could become a reality for you, too. Besides, you need to get married so you can have sex privileges, because men who don't, well, they . . . turn out kind of strange . . ."

As the summer wore on, listening to my aunt and uncle's easy jocularity with the customers, I often wondered if she could have any idea of how hard I had tried to conquer my shyness, how handicapped I was by it, and how miserable my shyness made me feel.

Having sewn on the missing buttons, Father Alfonse hands my coat back to me. I thank him. As I climb the basement steps, I am still worrying that I have imposed on him.

At the top of the steps, I hear a voice call softly. It's Father Alfonse. I walk back down the stairs. "Did you call me?"

"Would you like this?" he replies shyly, holding out an apple.

"No thank you," I tell him, feeling that his kindness in sewing on the buttons is enough.

"Tomorrow is a day of fasting," he says, hesitantly.

"It is? You mean we won't get anything to eat?"

"Yes, but nothing between meals."

"I'll take the apple," I tell him. I feel as if I've made a friend.

"Father Alfonse is very shy, isn't he?" I say to Father Bede afterwards. "But I like him."

"Yes, he is. He was a prisoner of war and had a lot to contend with. But he doesn't have to talk if he doesn't want to. We're no ladies' social club. We respect each other's rights to inner privacy. We just offer him our love."

Father Bede understands Father Alfonse, and I respect him for it.

*Anger and mistrust mark almost any initial encounter
with a stranger*

I get my first real chance to know Brother Frank, a man whose presence I am always aware of, when I am sitting in front of the fire in the friary one evening. I'll never forget that dinner during one of my first days at the monastery, when I forgot the hand signal used to ask for the meat. Brother Frank, who is handsome, and ruggedly built, with a solid walk, and quick, decisive movements, was seated next to me. He had noticed my hesitation and asked me in a whisper what I needed. I told him.

"This way," he had said, raising his open hand, then suddenly bringing it down like a judo chop, so it struck the table with a jolting whack, "like you're breaking a man's neck."

Food spilled, I jumped, coffee slopped, and dishes rattled. Father Burkhart had jerked his chair back, looked down at his plate, at the peas on the oilcloth, then up at Brother Frank.

"It's okay, Father," Brother Frank said. "You look well enough fed to me."

"We'll talk about that later," Father Burkhart shouted. "Leave the table. That's an order."

"Much later," Brother Frank said, laughing to himself. Then he got up, pushed his chair in, and carried his dishes out to the kitchen.

I had sat there for several minutes waiting for my hands to steady so I could finish my coffee.

Now, Brother Frank is silently pacing back and forth behind me in the friary, as I've seen him do before. The others are down in the recreation room and we are alone.

Suddenly he comes over and sits down on the other end of the deacon's bench.

"What are *you* doing here?" he asks.

"I'm a friend of Father Bede's."

"Father Bird, huh?" Brother Frank laughs at his own joke.

"I've been going with him to visit some of the poor Spanish families that he's trying to help. He told me that you're an auto mechanic, and he hopes you can help him fix up the old bus in the yard to use for trips for some of the boys and girls."

"Yes, I could help him. But he really took some liberties with the vow of obedience this time. Father Burkhart told him either to get it running, get rid of it, or move into it," Brother Frank says. "But I asked you what you're doing here." He speaks softly but he has an intense, decisive manner. If I knew then what was going to happen four months later, I might have asked him the same question.

"My car broke down and I was out of money. I came here just to spend the night and Father Bede invited me to stay on. I'm glad I did, too. I like it here."

"Father Bede said that you spent some time in Denver."

"Yes, I did. Do you know Denver?"

"I lived there a while. Do you know where Duffy's Irish Bar is?"

"Yes, I've been there; have you, too?"

Brother Frank nods. "Have you ever been in the Pink Elephant?"

"No."

"The Mirror Lounge?"

"No."

"The Carousel?"

"No, just Duffy's, of those you mention. Do you know where the Rode Hotel is? That's where I worked. And I worked part time for a Japanese outdoor market on South Broadway, too, 'Farm Fresh Gardens.' "

The dusty smell of the canvas awning and rotting watermelon on a hot summer day comes back to me. And the old woman who told me, 'You're standing on my foot, get off it or I'll piss on your leg.' And the young toughs, arms covered with crude, homemade, indelible ink tattoos, would buy cherries in cones of rolled up newspaper, then stand around spitting the pits at passersby on the sidewalk.

"A young guy like you should be out having a good time," Brother Frank says. "Drinking beer. Having fun with people your own age. Living it up. Chasing the girls. Father Bede told me about that rooming house full of derelicts and pathetic old men you lived in. What attracted you to them?"

"I lived there because it was cheap. There would've been all girls if I'd had my choice, but there were only old men, nothing to 'chase.' "

I had felt sorry for the elderly men living alone in their small rooms or cramped efficiencies. I discovered how appreciative old people are of the companionship of a young person my age, especially if you listen sympathetically. They often had interesting things to tell about their past lives, which I enjoyed. We helped each other; they trusted me and I trusted them. They were kind and compassionate.

Trying to draw the conversation away from myself, I ask Frank, "How long have you been here at the monastery, Father?" having assumed he is a priest.

"Don't call me 'Father,' " he says sharply. "I'm *not* a priest. You can call me Frank, or Brother Frank, I don't have a religious name."

"You wear a habit, though."

"But not the hood. Non-religious brothers wear the habit, but we're not permitted to wear the hood."

I ask him what a non-religious brother is.

"I'm married. I have a wife and kids in Denver. But I *was* a priest. I was an Episcopalian priest for two years."

"And then you quit and joined the Catholics?"

"No. I was raised in the Catholic faith. Have you heard of the Trappists? I was a Trappist monk for five years. But I had to leave. I busted a priest in the mouth. I have a weakness for poker, and he didn't like it. He gave me no choice."

"Father Bede told me you were in the Marines during World War II."

"That's right. I won two Congressional Medals of Honor. You can look it up in the Congressional Record. After the war I went to Italy and joined the underworld. I lived there two years. Why haven't you been drafted yet?"

"I'm 4-F, but I was in the Air Force R.O.T.C. when I was in college. It was compulsory and I hated it."

I could never learn the maneuvers—'column left,' 'column right,' 'parade rest,' and so on. I was too nervous and uncoordinated. The only way I could do the maneuvers was to watch the guy on my left or right and do what he did, so I was always a step or two behind.

Brother Frank looks at me. "I should've had you in my platoon during the war," he says. "I could take boys away from their mothers, show them how to stay alive, teach them a dozen ways to kill a man, send them into combat, and make men out of them. I could've made a man out of you."

I am so angry and stunned that I can't talk for several minutes. I want to keep myself under control. "If that's the way you make men out of boys, it stinks," I choke out finally.

"I don't think you'll ever have any guts or backbone."

"Oh shit," I blurt out. I jump up and walk out and go back to my room and go to bed. I lie awake for a long time, hating Brother Frank's guts, angry at myself for confiding in him. I wonder how I can avoid him and how I'll face him in the morning.

"Bill, yer've made a good friend in Brother Frank, yer 'ave," Brother Patrick tells me the next morning after breakfast, as we meet in the friary.

"I have? Really?" That certainly comes as a surprise.

He asks me what we talked about.

"We've both been in Denver; we talked about that and other things."

"Did ya talk about bars?"

I tell him yes, Brother Frank asked me what bars I'd been in.

"Don't talk about bars to Frank, Bill."

"Okay, but why not?"

"Frank came 'ere six months ago. He was bummin' around 'n' 'e came to the convent in Laro, worked a while for the sisters, 'e did, 'n' t'ey sent 'im up 'ere ta Father Burkhart. 'E's an alcoholic 'n' Father Burkhart made 'im take the Pioneer Pledge of the Sacred 'eart. 'E hasn't touched a drop since!"

"Brother Frank's had it rough," Father Bede adds, joining us. "I told you he's a Marine combat veteran, and his experiences during the war still disturb him. He can't reconcile them. There are some things I could tell you about him that you might not believe, but I can't. I'm trying to help him."

Suddenly I'm aware that I don't have my coat (now stained

with oil and gas from my chain saw). I go back up to the refectory to look for it, but it isn't there. I go back down to the friary and ask Father Bede if he's seen it. "I'm sure I left it on the back of my chair at breakfast, but it's not there now. Is somebody playing a trick on me?"

"No, Bill, I think Brother Frank has it. Check the laundry room."

I go down to the basement and there he is on his hands and knees with a scrub board, rubbing the spots out of it.

"Thanks, Brother Frank," I say. "I should've done that."

"Yes, you should've, but you didn't. Don't worry about it."

Some mornings later, I wake up with the flu and don't go to breakfast. There is a knock on my door and it's Brother Frank with an orange and a piece of corn bread wrapped up in a napkin.

"Are you all right, Bill?" he asks. "I'm just checking up on you. I worried when you didn't come to breakfast."

I tell him I'm going to stay in bed. He goes to his cell and comes back with a small reading lamp which he nails above my bed. Then he goes out and brings back some aspirin. "Take these," he says, "and any time you need them, there's a bottle on my dresser. Just go in and help yourself; it doesn't matter if I'm there or not."

I know by now that a monk's cell is his only private place, his sanctuary and refuge.

"Thank you, Brother Frank."

"I hope you feel better."

By afternoon I do feel better. After supper while the others are at recreation, Brother Frank and I sit down in the friary to talk. I ask him where he grew up.

"On the tough south side of Boston. When I went off to school, I had to pack a bicycle chain in my lunch pail instead of a sandwich."

Brother Frank has huge biceps. He has a submarine tattooed on his chest and others on his arms. "I like your tattoos," I tell him.

"I'd like to get one. I saw a bum in a bar in Denver who had a list of every major city he'd been in tattooed the entire length of his arm: 'I love Palm Beach, 1949,' was at the top."

"I had them put on during the war, so if I got my head blown off they could still identify the body," he snaps.

After the war, Brother Frank tells me, he worked as a commercial fisherman: "We'd fish all day, then at night we'd go out and rob oyster beds. I hadn't been shot at since the war, and it was hard getting used to it again. I'd listen to the waves and they'd say, 'We'll get you, Frank, we'll get you.'"

He and a Marine friend pooled their life's savings, borrowed some money and bought a fishing boat. "It was the dream of a lifetime," Brother Frank says. "I got drunk one night and broke it up on a coral reef. I couldn't go near the water after that."

Brother Frank has a tough exterior but a compassionate heart. He adopts all the stray cats that are dumped off at the monastery during the night. He strokes them and feeds them and shinnies up trees to rescue them. With his powerful arms and shoulders he is as agile as a cat. When he climbs up a tree, the other brothers stop what they are doing and come out and gather around to watch.

I try to reconcile his gentleness, kindness, and his willingness to listen with the violent things he tells me about his background.

He and Brother Thomas, the lanky young printer from Indianapolis, can never see eye to eye. "He doesn't know what life is really like," Brother Frank tells me. "I'd like to take him out behind the barn and kick him in his diaper rash."

I gather that Father Burkhart somehow also figures in this because he and Brother Thomas are blood brothers, and Brother Frank resents authority, one can easily see that.

On the other hand, one morning when Brother Thomas was in bed with the flu, the steam jet popped off his radiator, making a racket and filling the room with steam. Brother Patrick and Father Burkhart poked their heads in the door and just stood there, but Brother Frank wrapped his hand in a towel, went in, found the steam jet and put it back on. Then, while we watched, he carried out an armload of wet books and came back with dry sheets and blankets.

Brother Thomas didn't even nod or say thank you.

The bell gongs for Complin and Brother Frank and I head for the chapel.

"It was good talking to you, Frank. I hope we can do it again."

"We will."

"The more we are rejected by others, the more we consent to God" — Father Bede

By the end of the month I begin to feel that I have three good friends, Father Bede, Brother Frank, and Father Alfonse. But among the others I still feel like an intruder.

One day a gray-haired priest from Albuquerque drops by and stays for lunch. Everyone is cordial, and Father Burkhart, who is usually gruff and taciturn, tells a dirty story and laughs so hard he chokes.

The visitor leaves. At the dinner table that evening Brother Patrick raises his hand and asks for permission to speak:

"Our visitor," he begins shyly, rising, "asked me to convey 'is t'anks to all of you, 'e did, 'n' ta say good-bye."

"Good-bye," Father Burkhart sneers.

"Hurry back real soon," Brother Vincent says, laughing.

"Yeah, drop in anytime," Brother Thomas adds.

I am stunned. I didn't know monks talked that way; I thought they were more charitable. Father Bede didn't say anything, neither did Patrick or Frank, that was some relief. Why were the others so sarcastic? He seemed gentle and kind, and I feel sorry for him.

I feel rejected, too. They must feel the same way toward me. Would they rather I leave? Would they say the same things about *me*?

I go back to my room to try to figure things out. I painfully go over every happy moment at the monastery. I hadn't realized until now how wrapped up I have become in my new life. Dozing off, I awake with a start. Father Bede has told me I can stay. Father Burkhart has, too, in so many words. I want to. I have to.

Two nights later two scruffy Jesuits, unshaven and with ragged crew cuts, their gray habits spotted, come to visit and share the room adjoining mine. They don't know I am next door and they chatter away like pine squirrels half the night.

"Look at all the broken plaster, you can even see the lathes."

"I wonder how long since they swept this place! This window is full of cobwebs."

"And curls of dust under the bed. I hope the sheets are clean. Boy, wait 'till we get back and tell the Jesuits about *this* place. I'm beat. Good night. Hey, who's that young kid, anyway? He sure doesn't get paid for talking, does he. What's *he* doing here?"

"Father Burkhart says he's just some fly-by-night kid they're stuck with. 'Father Bede's Misfit,' he calls him."

That hurts. I jerk my suitcase out from underneath the bed and begin stuffing my clothes into it.

But by the time my suitcase is packed, I've calmed down a little and have begun to reconsider. I can't stand the thought of leaving. And I can't run out on a man who has been as good to me as Father Bede.

The next morning when I meet him in the friary, he asks, "How are your Jesuit neighbors? Did they sleep well?"

"I guess so, they slept through Mass," I reply.

"Did you get acquainted?"

"No, I don't really want to."

"Why not?"

I tell him what the Jesuit brothers said.

"I *like* misfits, Bill, I don't like 'fits.' Don't feel bad about that, feel good about it. We're all misfits here. Don't you see that anyone who rejects the materialism of this world, where success is measured by the amount of money you earn and the prestige of your position, where compassion and love for others is a sign of weakness, where there is so much indifference to hurt and suffering, is a misfit in the eyes of the world? We don't fit into that world, you and I don't, none of us here does. We reject it. The word 'misfit' should be a comfort to you, as it is to me.

"Brother Frank wants Deaf Don to teach you some boxing skills. He thinks it would give you more confidence. You do what you want. But don't believe that Old Testament stuff about an eye for an eye. In the past, Brother Frank has sometimes used it as a justification for punching people in the mouth. Remember, you conquer others with love, not swords. It's not so important to be tough; people who are bullies can hurt your body or wound your pride, but they can't take away your soul."

Father Bede leaves; he says he has some things to talk over with Father Burkhart.

I go upstairs to the refectory for a cup of coffee and to ask Deaf Don about the possibility of some boxing lessons, when I run into Brother Frank. "Bring your coffee downstairs; let's sit in front of the fire where it's warmer," he says.

I tell him what the Jesuit brothers said.

"What do they know about life? What did you say to them?"

"Nothing, Frank."

"Did you tell Father Bede? What did he say?"

"He always says to love others and forgive them."

"Coo, coo, good ol' Father Bird," Brother Frank says. "Why don't you talk up? Is it because you're too kind, or are you afraid?"

"A little of each," I reply.

"If you *are* afraid, there are bastards who can sniff out fear and weakness the way a dog does. They're all around us in this world, even the Bible says so: 'Dogs have encompassed me. Deliver my soul from the power of the dog,' " he quotes.

"It happens all the time with me, encounters, I mean, with those 'bastards' you're talking about," I tell him. "In school, in bars, in a factory I worked in, in that hotel in Denver. It's my manner. I've never had any confidence in myself. I can't talk up or assert myself. It's humiliating. I can't express the rage and self-loathing I feel because of it. I don't have any friends because I'm too uneasy around people. And I can't last out a job, any job. Once I clerked in a photo store. If you made a mistake the boss took it out of your wages. One morning when I came to work he handed me my pay check and said, 'Wait till you see *your* check this week!'

"I panicked, grabbed my coat and ran out the back door without saying anything. Just the thought of opening the envelope threw me. Finally, after two days, I tore it open to see how much he had deducted. Nothing. He had added a nice commission for a camera sale I'd made."

"Why didn't you check it out with him in the first place?" Brother Frank asks.

"I couldn't. You can let it, anger I mean, get the best of you, wear you down, obsess you day and night. And let it stymie you at every turn until you feel as if you can't function, can't deal with people, can't hold onto a job, can't do anything."

"If you let it do *that*, you *are* a cripple," Brother Frank says. "Carrying all that anger around in your guts that way, keeping it all inside, letting it eat you up, that's what makes you so tense and nervous, isn't it? That and being afraid someone is going to say something that's going to wound or injure you. Well, I'm your friend and I don't mean to say anything that might hurt you. As your friend, I wish I could help you."

"I'd like to be able to handle my anger the way you sometimes do."

"What do you mean by that?" he asks.

"Well, I listen to you and Father Bede after supper at night when you're sitting in the friary and talking, all your stories of how you got even with this person or that person. I'm asking, Brother Frank, because I'd really like to know."

"Know what?" he snaps. "What are you talking about?"

"Well . . . ." I wish I hadn't gotten myself into the spot I'm in. "How you nearly beat to death that drill instructor in the Marines who had it in for you. And how you stayed around for years just to make life miserable, as you put it, for that doctor who mis-diagnosed the illness of that young boy, a friend of yours, who didn't have the flu the way the doctor said he did and hemorrhaged to death because his bowels were blocked. And that priest you slugged."

"I saw a hell of a lot more of the world by the time I was your age than you'll see in a lifetime."

"I know, Brother Frank, that's true. But my angers are just as real to me as yours are to you."

"But you hold your anger in. You keep it buried in your guts."

"Yes, I do, but sometimes I can't. When I get angry, I feel it build up in minutes, until I think the pressure will explode through the top of my head. I get this sharp, almost paralyzing pain in my lower back, my heart feels as if *it* will explode, and I have to gasp for breath. If I let my anger out, I lose complete control."

" 'And he was such a nice boy, so quiet and polite,' " Brother Frank says in a mocking tone of voice. "That's how the newspapers will quote your landlady someday after you've been hauled off to prison. Can you use your fists if you have to?"

"I hit a guy once. I hurt him, and later I was sorry. There've been lots of times I wanted to and didn't."

I tell Brother Frank about the man at the hotel. ". . . . Then he said, 'Let's go down to the men's room, fart.' If I could've killed him, I would have. He was bigger than I was. I didn't even know what to say. I turned around and walked away and he called after me, 'Let me know if you change your mind, fart.' That was one of the most humiliating things that ever happened to me . . ."

"Don't worry," Brother Frank says, "I might have done the same thing, just turned around and walked away. On the other hand, I probably wouldn't have."

"Well, later in the evening I heard a commotion in the rear lobby near the bar. A salesman had gotten into a fight with the bartender. The bartender had pushed the salesman face first into a plate-glass door, and he was lying on his back unconscious when I got there. His face was a bloody pulp, nose broken, but I recognized him."

"It was the same guy?"

"Yes, the same one."

"How did that make you feel?"

"After my initial shock it made me feel good."

"You got so angry at that salesman because he confirmed your own feelings about yourself, that you are a fart. And because you couldn't stand up to him the way you wanted to or think a man should. But he was the one with the problem, not you. You're no fart, you ought to know that."

"It's not just a problem with bastards like that guy," I say. "It's also that I can't argue or even discuss things calmly, I can't defend or assert myself, even in the most simple situations, because right away I feel tightness, panic, and anger and I can't think or talk straight. Afterwards I feel angry at the other person and angry at my helplessness."

"Don't worry about what other people might think or say about you," Brother Frank says, "because no one gives a damn about you, or about anyone else . . . except himself. Do what you want and say what you want and don't let anyone push you around.

"Don't you pray, the way Father Bede tells you? I watch you. You're very amenable to anything he tells you, you listen raptly and nod your head, but do you do what he tells you? If you don't, *nothing* will save you."

"I do pray. I'll keep trying. It helps to talk to you, Brother Frank."

"You're my friend, Bill. Don't forget it."

That evening, Brother Frank knocks on my door and asks me why I'm not at recreation. That really surprises me. I have assumed that I am excluded from their activities.

"I've never been invited," I tell him. "Besides, Father Burkhart always seems gruff towards me. He might not like it."

"You go," he says sharply. "If they don't want you there they'll tell you to leave, and you can leave."

I go over to the friary and down to the recreation room, stand there a minute and then knock.

"Yeah, who is it?" Father Burkhart yells.

I open the door and all eyes look up. Brother Thomas is spinning a country-western song on his dime-store record player. Father Bede is sitting by himself at the far end of the room reading a book. Brother Patrick is playing chess by himself and Father Burkhart is shuffling and reshuffling a deck of cards.

"What do you want?" Father Burkhart asks.

"Do you mind if I come in?" I say.

"I guess not. Do you play Hearts?"

"I played it once or twice when I was a kid."

"Grab a chair, you're going to play. Come on Vincent, Patrick, Brother Thomas."

I sit down nervously but I keep my wits, watch the others, and soon the game comes back to me.

Everything goes all right until the fifth round. Diamonds have been led. Father Burkhart slaps down the jack of diamonds, the highest card on the table.

My turn is next and I am the last man. I lay down the queen of spades.

"Oh shit!" Father Burkhart snorts, slamming down his cards. "Are you damn sure you don't have a diamond in your hand?"

Brother Vincent coughs hard trying to cover a laugh.

"Shit!" Father Burkhart repeats, glaring at him.

"You've been drafted," Brother Frank tells me later. "From now on it's Hearts, for the rest of your stay here. Father Burkhart is a sore loser. He'll never forgive you. He won't have peace until he's paid you back. And remember, when you play hearts with Father Burkhart, don't ever try to leave the table until the game is over."

"Or give him the black queen again, right?" I add. "When Father Burkhart swore, it startled me. I didn't expect him to do that."

Brother Frank laughs. "Father Burkhart has been known to use an expletive or two."

I was six or seven when I first heard the word 'shit.' I was walking home from school with my friend Teddy Terrill. A girl rode by on a bicycle and Teddy shouted at her, "Shit, ass!" I was shocked. I knew they were bad words but didn't know what they meant. When I got home I asked my father. He took me up to his study. He told me that the word 'shit' was another word for bowel movement; it was a naughty word and I should never use it.

I asked him about 'ass.' He said, " 'Ass' is just another word for 'donkey.' "

"How can one thing have two names?"

"It just does, that's all," Dad said.

It was astonishing to me that two different words could each mean the same thing.

I said, "Dad, that's a good riddle: What's the difference between an ass and a donkey? Nothing! They're the same thing!"

My father said, "All right, but don't use the word 'shit.' "

The next morning we had 'show-and-tell.' To my chagrin, I had never been able to offer anything worth-while to show-and-tell. Demonstrating a paper clip had been my biggest dud. But finally I thought I really had something exciting to contribute. Memorizing, as always, was a great problem for me, but I had rehearsed my riddle over and over.

When it was my turn, I got up, trembling, but aware that I had something startling to reveal:

"I have a riddle," I said. "What's the difference between an ass and a donkey?"

I waited. There was silence. No hands went up, but my teacher looked interested, so did my friend, Teddy.

It was time for the answer. I froze. My mind was blank. I groped desperately. Finally, I had it: " 'Shit,' " I said.

"Oh, my, no, Bill, we do not use that word, ever!" my teacher scolded, setting off shrieks from the other children.

*"You'll like Brother Patrick, but he's as irresponsible as
a shin-kicking school boy"* — Brother Frank

Early the next morning a loud rap on my door tumbles me out
of bed. I can't imagine who it is. Brother Patrick stands there, greasy
cowboy hat with wide, floppy brim and baggy trousers with the fly still
safety-pinned, asking if I would like to help him gather firewood. He
doesn't have to ask twice.

"Ah, t'anks, t'anks, friend," he says.

I like Brother Patrick's rough looks, his flattened nose, his
ruddy complexion, his sloppy clothes, his brogue, and the tall shock of
black hair that stands straight up in the middle of his head, perfect
cover, I think, for a covey of quail. I also like his shy, wistful manner.

"Watch out for ol' Patrick," Brother Frank has warned me.
"Don't let his shyness fool you; if he gets to know you, he'll talk your
ears off. Don't ever believe a word he says. He's supposed to tip loaves
in the bakery like the rest of us, but he thinks he's Teddy Roosevelt,
and he'd rather conquer the great outdoors in that ridiculous cowboy
hat. Father Burkhart will catch up with that guy one of these days."

It's a job for the two of us, Patrick and me, to push the big truck, a lopsided, five-ton Mack without windshield, doors, or right-front fender, out of the shed, so we can haul the firewood in it. Brother Patrick has to fill the leaky radiator and add two or three quarts of bulk oil. Then he lets the truck coast down the incline, pops the clutch to turn the engine over, and off we go, jerking and rattling down the cowpath behind the barn, clattering across the cattle guard, and down through the pasture, trailed for a quarter of a mile ("Look back 'n' see where we've come!" he shouts) by huge clouds of steam from the radiator.

We have picked up good speed by the time we hit the woods near the river and we never slow. We plow into the woods, weaving through the trees, bouncing over stumps and fallen timber, the truck rocking, the radiator erupting, the five-gallon bucket between my knees, full of water when we started out, almost empty now and my clothes soaked, the windowless cab full of leaves and broken branches, with Brother Patrick yelling every time my head meets the metal roof of the cab, "Did ya 'it yer 'ead 'ard?"

"How hard do you mean?" I ask, exasperated.

"Well, friend, did ya t'ink we'd make it?" he asks finally, grinning at me.

"I was hoping we would," I reply.

"That Patrick is completely reckless," Brother Frank warns me, coming up to me in the friary that evening and grabbing my shoulder, "and he's even worse when he has an audience. You stay away from him. He's going to kill himself and you, too, if you ride with him."

But gathering firewood with Brother Patrick becomes an almost daily, early morning occurrence.

Brother Patrick swings the double-bitted axe wildly, with the same insane intensity with which he drives the truck. I stand well out of his way. He doesn't want to use my chain saw. He chops the heavy limbs into six-foot lengths and I stand them on end, balance them across my shoulder and tip them into the Mack. If I slow, Brother Patrick spurs me on: "Ah, I've got a feelin' yer a wee bit delicate." And then, when I hurry: "Ah, Bill, ya got a stout back, ya 'ave! T'at's a real lorry load. T'anks, t'anks."

Then we rest. "Bill, you 'n' I, we're just a bunch of woolly bums, but we make a good team, we do; you were always workin' alone, 'n' I t'ought ya might be lonesome fer a wee bit of company. We both like workin' outdoors. 'N' from now on neither one of us will have to work alone. I could use yer 'elp in the afternoons, too, Bill. T'ere's a lot of handywork waitin' for us around 'ere."

"Woolly bums, that's us," I say, happily.

After an afternoon of sun and hard work he sighs wearily over our game of checkers at evening recreation: "Ah, Bill, a lit-le work, a lit-le prayer, a lit-le fun, fer ta make a balanced life."

Sore throats, raw weather, crossed candles—go together

By the end of the fifth week the weather turns damp and raw. There is a rap on my door before breakfast one morning.

"Who is it?" I ask.

"It's BumbleBede, can't you hear the hum?" He asks me to drive into Laro with him. He wants to bless throats at the convent school.

We shove boxes of mended toys and old clothes in the back of the bakery truck. I find a pair of small cowboy boots. "I wonder if these would fit Earlito?" I ask. "Can I give them to him?"

"You sure can."

"I've got some polish in my room, be right back."

Then Father Bede jumps behind the wheel. We fly down the mountain, every nut, bolt, and breadcrumb, Father Bede singing and pounding the steering wheel, sail over a bump and land so hard the truck bottoms out. Toys fly everywhere. The tailpipe, torn loose, clatters against the pavement all the way into Laro, making a terrible racket. Father Bede, behind the wheel, is almost as reckless as Brother Patrick.

"You've got a lead foot, too, just like Patrick," I tell him. "But I like you both well enough to risk my neck. Patrick's a long way from Dublin and his father's pub; how did he happen to come to the monastery?"

"In a fancy Hillman Minx, in the same kind of hurry. He landed in New York and was going to California to see his brother. He picked up a hitchhiker who was as base and depraved as the Devil himself. He gave Patrick the cold sweats. After four-hundred miles with him, Patrick was so disturbed he needed a spiritual retreat, and he stopped at the Abbey in Flint, Michigan, and asked if he could stay a few days. The Abbot, with a tear in the corner of his eye, said, 'Oh Patrick, we need you, we need you!'

"The Abbot needed someone to paint a house. It turned out to be a house with forty people in it. Patrick took one look at it and said, 'Well, if I'm going to paint *that*, I might just as well stay.' And stay he did. He took his perpetual vows, and the Abbot sent him to us. He drove up here in that fancy Hillman Minx."

"He must have hustled a lot of ale in his father's pub for that one," I say.

"Father Burkhart was gone and I was in charge. I hated to take it away from him, but you know our vow of poverty. The sisters at the convent needed transportation and I gave it to them. They ran it out of oil and we had to scrap it. Poor Patrick!"

When we get to Laro, Father Bede tells me: "The others think my Mass is innovative and far out. 'Hold your hands just twelve inches apart, and make an 'O' with your thumb and forefingers, so you don't trail any impurities.' Don't they know that when Christ carried the cross up Calvary they stepped in His blood and trailed it all over?"

When we walk into the church, I feel all eyes on me. Father Bede and I are the only Anglos.

Father Bede says Mass. Then he tells the congregation of adults and children: "Today, don't come to confession to tell me you have done something bad. I only want to hear your confession if you have had a chance to do good, to help someone, or to be kind."

There are several rows of benches near the altar forming a semi-circle, where the children sit. The adults sit behind them in the pews. On the floor in front of the altar is a wire basket with a hand-lettered sign taped to it, "Food For The Poor." Almost every child holds a can of food.

Father Bede makes up a story for the children about a boy who jumps into a rapids to save a drowning girl. It becomes more and more dramatic as he goes along. The moral is to forget about yourself and help others. But the children become preoccupied with their cans of food. The largest is a half-gallon can of pineapple chunks, the smallest is a four-ounce can of tomato paste. One boy puts his can of soup on the floor and noisily rolls it back and forth with his foot, until the label comes off. Another boy tries to balance a can of pears on his head. Other children are tossing their cans into the air and catching them. Occasionally Father Bede's sermon is punctuated by the loud "thunk" of a can hitting the floor.

The sermon over, the children rush up grinning proudly and noisily toss their cans into the basket.

"Thank you, children," Father Bede says. "Now line up so I can bless your throats." As they step forward one at a time, Father Bede holds two heavy crossed candles at each throat with the "V" touching the Adam's apple and gives a blessing. The children grin up at him and he smiles back.

When we are done, Father Bede says, "Well, Bill, we skinned that cat; grab the basket and let's slip out of here."

"Who is the food for?" I ask.

"Put it in the truck. It's for Mrs. Cortez. Her husband died two months ago and she's in the hospital, with seven children to feed and an eleven year old daughter taking care of them and running the household."

As we are leaving, one of the nuns rushes up and says, "Oh, Father, some of the sisters are ill. Please bless *their* throats." So we go to the convent. I am taken with a little nun named Laura and ask Father Bede about her.

"She may not make it. She's having a difficult time. She's so rigid and duty-bound. O-bey, o-bey, o-bey! I'd like to throw my arms around her and give her a big kiss. Just for starters, that is."

"What do you think she'd do?" I ask.

"She'd stop a minute, tingle, and then she'd run clear to the Pope."

I laugh and Father Bede roars. "With a slight head start I'd be waiting for her when she got there," I say. "She sure is cute."

We stop to deliver the canned food to the Cortez home. Then Father tells me that Tony, the young man to whom he had given some carving tools, has something to show us and we drive up the hill to Tony's house.

Tony has carved a miniature covered wagon about a foot in length, pulled by a pair of yoked oxen, perfect in detail down to their ears and horns, broad backs and big round bellies. The wooden wheels on the wagon turn and have wooden spokes.

"Bless you, Tony, this is amazing," Father Bede exclaims. We get down on the floor on our hands and knees to admire it.

"Carry it out to the truck very carefully, Bill, buddy."

"I know some wealthy people who will buy it," he says, when we are in the truck. "I want to start some small craft industries around here to help these people, and I want your help. We have Tony. I can sell everything he carves. I know of a woman who does beautiful weaving. I know of a man who makes pottery. And the Corrillo sisters. I've been selling their miniature grottoes to a store in Carlsbad. And I'd like to start some craft classes for the children. We'll turn the porter's lodge into a shop. Tourists breeze through here in the summer."

Father Bede's enthusiasm is contagious. I have seen the impoverishment of the area, and I know of Father Bede's love for the Spanish people, his desire to help, and their respect for him. I'm happy that I am going to be involved.

Glancing at Tony's oxen and covered wagon that I'm holding on my lap, Father Bede whoops as we swerve around a corner. "Things are rollin', Bill! Let's swap that old Chevy of yours for a pair of oxen, so we don't have to add a quart of oil every time we drive it into town and back," he says.

"Maybe I'll hitch 'em to that old bus of yours and haul it away for Father Burkhart," I reply. "That would put me in his good graces."

We stop for gas. "Father, are you from the monastery?" the young girl-attendant asks.

"No, I'm from Oakabowka Heights," Father Bede says, laughing, still elated. "I'm Rosary Bede."

"Please bless my throat, Father. And my son is sick inside . . ."

"His kidney, liver, appendix?"

"What? No, inside, inside the house; will you bless his, too? Poppa, poppa, come and have the Father bless your throat."

Finally, many throats later, we are on our way back to the monastery, loping along the narrow mountain road, Father Bede behind the wheel again, singing, and I, bracing myself against the dash and braking with my feet.

"That pair of cowboy boots sure made Earlito happy," Father Bede says. "His face was as bright as the shine you put on them."

"A little Kleenex stuffed in the toes helped the fit. I hope living with those other children will draw some of the fear and hurt out of him."

Supper is on the table when we get back. Suddenly, Father Bede seems weary. "I can't eat," he says. "My throat has begun to hurt."

"The two of you together don't have the brains God gave an avocado" — Father Burkhart

Brother Patrick is proud of an old bicycle he found in the barn, part of the accumulation of toys and clothes for the poor that Father Bede collected in Carlsbad. Father Bede let Brother Patrick have it, perhaps in part making up for having to take away his Hillman Minx.

Now it has a headlight off a jeep, its heavy battery attached to the fork with miles of friction tape, a lady's hand mirror fastened to the handlebars, and a pair of fringed, leather saddlebags, falling apart and green with mold. Brother Patrick had done the vow of poverty proud.

The other brothers have to walk back and forth from the bakery to the friary, but Brother Patrick sails by them on his bicycle.

On still mornings, after a snow has fallen during the night, he's out in the yard in front of the friary at daybreak, before breakfast, trying to spin circles on his bicycle like a kid.

And when the snow has melted, he's down in the pasture on his bicycle chasing the horses for fun, waving his cowboy hat.

When we change the bed linen, it is only a hop, skip, and kerplunk from the laundry room door to the cells in the courtyard, but no matter: The folded linen fits nicely across the handlebars, the saddlebags are a good place for the soap and wash rags, and the handle of a broom holds eight rolls of toilet paper. When he is steadied, I give him a push and off he wobbles, one hand guiding the bicycle, the other hand balancing the broom handle in the air.

"'Ere, Bill, you try it this time," he insists.

I had great difficulty learning how to coordinate mind and muscles, compared to my twin brother who could do things easily. When I was about three I got a new trike, but I couldn't learn how to ride it for three or four weeks. Then I discovered I could walk behind and push it along, my stomach on the seat and my hands on the handlebars. Eventually I mastered it.

When we were nine, my father bought us bikes for our birthdays. My brother jumped right on his and rode off. By that time I knew I'd have trouble, even with help, so I admired the color and, supposedly to protect it, put it carefully back in the garage where it stayed unused for weeks.

My father got it out one afternoon. He said, "Let's play a little," making a game out of it to relax me. Then he said—my father the professor—"I'll explain the theory of a bike to you. If you roll a tire down the highway, it stays upright, once it's rolling. A bike is the same way, there's centrifugal force in the spinning wheels. If a bicycle is moving forward, it stays upright. The minute it stops, it falls over. It's the forward motion that keeps it upright." Then he told me, "Get up on the seat, I'll hold the bike."

I climbed up on the seat and my father held me up until I was balanced. Then he gave me a good push and shouted, "There you go!"

The bike wove across our big yard and kept going. It sailed off a four-foot stone-wall embankment onto a sunken terrace, mangling the bike's front fender, bending the wheel rim and breaking spokes. I'd broken a bone at my elbow, and had to wear a long-arm cast.

"You can ride a bike, can't ya? Get on," he urges.

"Hey, don't push, Patrick!"

The bed linen ends up in the mud on the ground, just as Father Burkhart is on his way out to the road to pick up the mail.

I stand there, straddling the bicycle, hanging on to the broomstick with the rolls of toilet paper.

"What in the hell are you doing?" Father Burkhart asks, pointing at the ground.

"Airing it in public," I say under my breath to Brother Patrick.

"May I interrupt?" he asks.

"Sure, Father," Patrick replies, innocently.

"Bill, let the air out of both tires, all of it, until they're flat," Father Burkhart orders. "Brother Patrick, go get the tire pump and bring it to my cell immediately. Then the two of you put that damn bicycle back in the barn and leave it there. Get started."

After Father Burkhart has stomped off, we stand there for several minutes, shaken. "Let the air out?" I ask. "He really means it?"

Brother Patrick, pale, nods.

"I'm sorry about your bicycle," I tell him.

"Don't feel bad," he says, glum. "Father Burkhart has a quick temper, 'e does, like a fire springin' up, but 'e's a kind man."

"He was kind enough to let me stay here," I reply.

Suddenly we hear Brother Frank catching it, and look around. We can't see Father Burkhart, just hear him, but Brother Frank is perched high in the bare, upper-most branches of a tall tree near the bakery, trying to rescue a small cat, while the bakery ovens stand unattended.

Monastic obedience has ebbed.

Country-western music can once again be heard drifting from Brother Thomas's print shop, despite Father Burkhart's warning.

Father Alfonse is laid up with a bruised hip, having slipped in three inches of soapy water on the laundry-room floor, despite Father Burkhart's repeated warnings about using too much detergent.

And Father Bede, where-a-bouts known only to me, is napping in the back of his battered tour bus.

"I hear Father Burkhart had to punish Brother Patrick again," Brother Frank whispers to me at dinner.

"Again?" I ask.

"That guy's brains are always looking for the nearest exit."

"Well," I whisper, "he's great fun to be around."

Later that evening at recreation I ask Brother Patrick what he does in the bakery five mornings a week.

"Ah, friend, come over 'n' 'ave a good look for yerself," he tells me.

The next morning I go over to the bakery to watch.

Brother Vincent, the swarthy, rugged farmboy, always cheerful and easy-going, is in charge. He has taught himself how to use an old 8 × 10 camera that turned up in the accumulation of discards Father Bede has collected for the poor, set up a makeshift darkroom in the basement of the friary, and now some of his large black and white photographs, one a scene of the stark ruins of the mission church at the Pueblo, another of desert, mesas, and sky, are displayed on the bakery walls. They are stunning. In the evenings, while the others are at recreation, Brother Vincent is often busy at work in his darkroom. He seems pleased by my interest in and admiration for his photography and is teaching me how to develop film and use the darkroom enlarger. We are becoming good friends.

But now, Brother Vincent is mixing and kneading the dough in an electric drum. Honey and raisins have been added.

Each loaf of bread is baked in an individual tin, and Brother Frank and Brother Patrick load and unload the oven shelves.

Brother Frank, wearing gloves, reaches into the oven, removes a tin, tips the tin over, and the loaf of baked bread drops out upside down onto the short-handled wooden paddle held at the ready by Brother Patrick. Patrick flips the loaf like a pancake, catching it rightside up on the paddle, slides the loaf off his paddle onto a table an arm's length away, and has his paddle back in position ready to catch the next loaf. They do it very quickly without missing a beat or dropping a loaf.

One-eyed Ernie, the only outside hired help, feeds the loaves into a small machine that slices, wraps and seals the loaves. The wrapper is white with the side view of a hooded monk in black habit on it.

Ernie loads the bread into the bakery truck, and at the end of the day he drives the truck to Carlsbad and Hobbs, where the bread is sold in grocery stores. Brother Vincent has converted the truck to propane gas, because it is cheaper than gasoline at 35¢ to 40¢ per gallon. The large cylinder is attached to the underside of the truck.

Brother Patrick shows me how to stand in front of the oven and use the wooden paddle. I drop many loaves. Finally I get the hang of it, but Brother Patrick has disappeared.

The heat is intense. It gives my face and skin a sickly pallor, opens every pore on my arms to the size of a pin head making them very visible, and gives me a tremendous thirst.

The sweat glistens on Brother Frank's huge biceps and makes his tattoos stand out more vividly. The submarine tattoo, beautifully executed, floats across his powerfully developed chest. Brother Vincent has a set of weights in the barn and Brother Frank works out with them regularly.

At noon when I finish my work, Brother Vincent says, "Good job, Bill, will we see you tomorrow morning?"

Taken aback, I reply, "You mean I work tomorrow?"

Morning after morning I get up and drag myself to the bakery. My appetite sags and I sleep poorly. Thousands of loaves of bread float around in my dreams.

I long to be outdoors with Brother Patrick, cutting firewood, hauling trash, fixing things, and tearing around in the truck with him. More and more I tire of working in the bakery, but I don't want to complain; I don't want anyone to think I can't carry my own weight.

"Brother Vincent says you're doing an excellent job in the bakery," Father Bede tells me. "He says he's going to make a real baker out of you. Father Burkhart expresses his approval, too."

For a moment I am pleased, but at the same time I begin to feel panic. Father Bede's compliment is double edged; does it mean that the job is now expected of me? My eagerness to please Father Bede is as great as my distaste for the bakery.

"Why are *you* working here?" Brother Frank asks me finally on the tenth day as we are tipping loaves.

"Patrick attached you to it didn't he? He's trying to pass it off on you because he doesn't like to work here. He'd rather be outdoors. He has a way of getting out of anything he doesn't want to do. At first, Father Burkhart had him mixing batter. Patrick didn't like the job and he deliberately used so much honey you couldn't even lift a loaf of bread. He's completely irresponsible. Don't let him pull a fast one; go tell him you don't want his job."

Brother Frank's remarks jolt me, confirming my own earlier suspicions. What hurts even more than being duped is the thought that Brother Patrick might be tired of having me around.

"I'm going to talk to Brother Patrick," I tell Brother Frank, my tongue thick.

On the way to the friary I run into Father Burkhart. I tell him that if he doesn't mind, I'd like to quit working in the bakery.

"No one *asked* you to work in the bakery," he growls. "You're not indispensable around here, you know."

"I know that, Father Burkhart. I started out doing it as a favor for Brother Patrick . . ."

"You did *what?*"

"He loves to work outdoors. He loves to do the fixing up and repair. There's a lot of it to be done around here, isn't there? And Brother Patrick is very handy."

"*I* will be the one who decides what's good for Brother Patrick," he replies sharply.

Hurt by Father Burkhart's abruptness, I go on my way to look for Brother Patrick. I spot him over near the side entrance of the friary, dumping the trash into the truck for a trip to the dump. With each step my anxiety increases. How will he react? Will he be angry at me? I think of the fun we've had together. Is it true that he is using me? Am I causing a rift that could even get me expelled from the monastery?

When I reach Patrick, I take a deep breath. "Brother Patrick, I don't want to tip loaves anymore."

"Ah, friend," he says, "welcome back, yer true blue; I t'ought I lost ya ta the bakery, I did."

"You what? I think you . . . this is very hard for me to say . . . my hoarse is dry, I can't talk right . . ."

"Yer horse is what?"

"No, I mean my voice is dry. Oh, nuts, no, I mean my throat is dry, that's why I'm hoarse. I'm too stirred up . . ."

"Calm yerself, Bill. What's wrong?"

"I am calm, dammit! What I mean to say is, I feel used. I thought we were good friends. But I think you foisted that bakery job off on me because you didn't want it."

"No one was bendin' yer arm, Bill. Why didn't ya speak up?"

"I'm speaking up now. I thought we had a good friendship. I sure enjoyed it. You hurt me; I think you took advantage of our friendship."

"Bill, I t'ink yer a wee bit sensitive, ya are."

Provoked to my usual reaction, feeling rage, panic, rejection, and excruciating pressure, I turn around and walk away wobbly-legged, seeing myself in my mind's eye fleeing the monastery in despair, knowing that life for me is never going to be the same.

"Bill! Bill! Bill!" he calls.

Turning around and waving my arms, I shout, "First you tell me I'm a wee bit delicate, now you tell me I'm a wee bit sensitive. Go wee wee in your shorts!"

"Bill, don't get so angry, come 'ere, Bill, where are you going?"

"Away! Out of here! To a sockhop! Home! Back to Denver, I don't give a damn."

"Come back 'ere, don't leave, you'll regret it."

Calming down, I reconsider. "I feel a little better now," I say, trying to catch my breath.

"Bill, I've never seen you get so angry. Let's talk."

"Yes, let's. I don't want to leave."

"Bill, I t'ought ya liked the bakery. Brother Vincent said 'e couldn't 'ire better 'elp. 'E praises ya. 'E t'inks ya might want ta be a baker someday."

"Yeah, and I might want to be a carnival geek and swallow live mice someday, too," I reply.

Brother Patrick laughs gently. "I t'ought ya liked it in the bakery, but now I know different. T'anks for telling me. I'm sorry, I am, for the misunderstandin'."

"Let's forget it now, Brother Patrick," I tell him, vastly relieved. "I should've talked it over with you earlier instead of getting all steamed up."

"Are we friends, Bill?"

"Yes, good friends."

"Kicksides, isn't t'at what they called 'em in the wild West?"

"No, sidekicks."

"Ah, Bill, yer still my good helper, I hope. Come on, we got a lot ta catch up on. Ya left me a bit short-handed. Hey, ya missed some excitement, too. T'is very mornin'."

I follow him around to the side of the truck behind the cab.

"My God, where did you find it?"

"It found me," he says. "I was hikin' down the cowpath, I was, and t'ere was an eagle perched in the uppermost branches of t'at lone cottonwood down in the pasture. Saw me, 'e did, 'n' took flight, straight in me direction, wingspan as wide as the bed of the lorry, closer 'n' closer, 'n' ya could 'ear the thump, thump, thump of 'is feathered elbows hittin' 'is body with such force. Threw meself on the ground, I did, 'n' right over me 'ead 'e swooped, 'is talons bared like grappling hooks, close enough ta rip the flesh off me back."

"You could've been killed, Patrick! What happened then?" I ask.

"I dusted back to the monastery 'n' grabbed Father Burkhart's .30-06." Father Burkhart was in Laro and Patrick took the gun without asking.

"And the bird was still there?"

"Perched in the very same tree, 'e was, a threat to man 'n' beast . . ."

"The cows, you mean?" He nods. "Did he swoop at you again?"

"T'at 'e did, but 'e lighted on the ground t'is time, 'e did, not more t'an t'irty feet from where I stood . . ."

"Wow, and then?"

"'E gave me a mean look, Bill, 'n' started walkin' slowly towards me . . ."

Now, the bird lay in the back of the truck like so much refuse. "He's beautiful. 'Was,' I should say."

"Keep t'is under yer 'at, Bill."

"I promise. 'Loose lips sink ships,' right, Patrick? Well, the Corrillo sisters will go crazy with all those feathers. That'll keep 'em tying trout flies till the cows come home. The very cows whose endangered lives you spared this morning," I say, grinning, though not intending to make light of his harrowing experience.

Later that afternoon, Brother Frank and I are sitting in the friary, waiting for supper. "Well," he says, "you must have straightened Patrick out. Father Burkhart ordered him back to the bakery five mornings a week."

"Patrick and I are the best of friends." Brother Frank talks tough, but he is fond of Brother Patrick.

"I'm proud of you, Bill, you showed some spine today."

For the first time I had told someone how I felt. I hadn't held my anger in or run away. I had talked things out. It was a good feeling.

We climb the steps to the refectory for supper. Everything is back to normal, I think to myself as I shovel in a large scoop of mashed potatoes. Brother Patrick and I are friends again, and I won't have to spend any more mornings in the bakery, either. I feel a great sense of relief.

Our supper is suddenly interrupted by the visit of a man from the state fish hatchery six miles up the road.

"Has anyone seen the hatchery's pet eagle fly this way?" Father Burkhart asks after introducing him.

The blood rushes into my face and I quickly look down. When I dare sneak a glance at Brother Patrick, his face is so close to his plate all I can see is the top of his head.

It is evening. I lie there in bed, momentarily thinking about Denver, half-wishing I could be there to spend just this evening, to escape into anonymity, lose myself. To walk up and down the downtown streets; buy a half-pint to conceal in my jacket; sit in the bars.

But I don't really want to be in Denver or anywhere else. I want to be right here, at the monastery. I have found a world which I like, men whose values I respect and friendships I cherish, who have renounced the world, the only world I had formerly thought existed.

Even in a bleak and ravaged landscape, some beauty can be found

One morning after Mass, Father Bede and I drive to an old, dry lake bed to dig up and bring back some clay for the Corrillo sisters who live with their mother, father, younger brother, younger sister, and older brother in the mountains behind the monastery. For a year now, Father Bede has been taking clay to the older girls, Martha, Beverly, and Lisa, so they can make miniature grottoes which he sells at gift shops in Carlsbad and as far north as Albuquerque.

The dirt road to the lake bed is narrow and rutted.

"Geez, it's rough," I exclaim, worried about my old car.

"Watch the expletives," Father Bede warns.

Hundreds of acres of dry, cracked, blueish mud lie before us in a basin a half-mile wide and several miles long, surrounded by steep, desolate, barren hills, stripped of their timber, boulder-strewn and peppered with stumps, more bleak and vast than anything I have ever seen.

We park and sit silently for several minutes, the wind howling and buffeting the car, dark clouds rolling in the sky.

"Make a lot of noise so these crazy Spanish won't mistake us for deer and take pot-shots at us," Father Bede warns after we get out of the car.

He whoops as we dig up large chunks of the blue clay and lift them into the trunk. "That's a lot of grottoes," I say, anxiously watching the back end of my car sag under the weight. The wind is bitterly cold and our eyes water and our ears ache. The cold clay makes our hands swell.

"This blue clay is beautiful," I say, "and about as blue as my tail. I'm freezing. I wonder how deep this lake was at one time?"

Father Bede begins to sing: " 'How deep's the water, Mama, four feet high and rising.' " He has been listening to Brother Thomas's country-western records.

"No, Father, not 'deep,' it's how 'high's the water: 'How high is the water, Mama? Two feet high and rising. How high is the water, Papa? She said it's two feet high and rising. But we can make it to the road in a home made boat, 'cause that's the only thing we got left that'll float. It's already over all the wheat and oats. Two feet high and rising.' "

"Don't recite it, sing it, Bill!"

"I can't sing. But I'll tell you how I almost drowned. It was last winter. I drove down to Florida with my school-teacher, maiden aunt. She was on a month-long vacation. I needed to earn some money, so I put an ad in the paper for yard work and got a response from a Dr. Frinznager, who lived on Sarasota Bay. I put on a suit to make a good impression, and went to see him.

"Dr. Frinznager was eighty-six, feeble, half-deaf and half-blind. He took me outside to show me around and tell me what had to be done. Between his garage and the bay, where the yard was very narrow, his boxer had left a mess. Dr. Frinznager tracked right through it, but I stepped up on the sea wall to avoid it, tripped on a boat clip and fell into six feet of water.

"As I surfaced struggling, I saw Dr. Frinznager rounding the corner of the house, still gesturing and mumbling about the flora and the fauna. When I caught up with him, dripping, my shoes and socks full of muck, and told him what had happened, he said, 'Oh hell, don't worry about it, I drove off that damn sea wall on my riding mower once!' "

Father Bede laughs. "Walk on water, Bill; it's not firm but fun."

We hike across the lake bed and climb a hundred feet to the top of the steep, almost vertical bank, to investigate the stark ruins of an old stone saw mill. My leather soles keep slipping but Father Bede pulls me along on the other end of his walking stick.

"All Spanish are suspicious of Anglos," Father Bede reminds me as we drive up to the Corrillo house later. "They think we're all rich and want to take advantage of them."

"That's a wood house, not an adobe like all the others. It's small but well kept up. Even the paint is fresh. Looks like they're building an addition, too. They must be better off than most of the Spanish families around here. What does Mr. Corrillo do?" I ask.

"They're not typical. He was lucky enough to find a job as a guard at the prison in Nunn. He's energetic and works hard, and the whole family pitches in to try to make ends meet. The girls work on their craft projects after school to earn extra money. They're all bright-eyed, smart, lively girls. Wait till you meet them."

The rooming house in Denver was on the fringes of a Spanish-American neighborhood. The Spanish girls who paraded past the porch where I'd sit on hot summer afternoons when I got back from work were the most beautiful girls I had ever seen. But girls and sex, or even just talk and friendship, were inexorably inaccessible because of my extreme shyness and unease. And Spanish girls, from a different culture, were even more exotic and remote.

We knock and go in. No one in the family, not even the mother and father, looks at me, talks to me, or offers me a chair. But then Martha comes home from school, shiny black hair to her waist, snug-little blue-jeaned hips, blue blouse knotted above her flat stomach. She grabs up two-year old Karen, dusts off the seat with her handkerchief, and offers the chair to me. The others jabber in Spanish with Father Bede, but Martha smiles at me with her eyes.

Driving back to the monastery, all I can think about is Martha.

In the weeks that follow Father Bede becomes aware of how I feel. He is very kind; almost every evening he has an errand for me to run, and I hike up the mountain path to Martha's. "Here, Bill," he'll say, "I want you to take this typing paper up to the Corrillo's for Martha to draw on. She wants to be an artist." Or, "Martha is tying flies to sell to the trout fishermen. Take her these feathers I found." Or, "Take Martha some more clay."

I am always wary, knowing that her parents probably resent me as an Anglo. But Martha is thoughtful and kind and greets me warmly. "Thank you for breenging me the clay," she says. Or, "Can you stay a while, Bill?" Or, "I hope you comb back soon, will you?"

And when Martha's large, dark, bright eyes linger on mine, even at moments when we aren't talking, I stand there unable to move, think, or speak.

But whenever I come to see Martha, her ten-year old brother, Felix, comes around and tries to spoil things. He jumps and clowns around, makes faces, jibberjabbers and pesters us, trying to be the center of attention.

Or he climbs on a dilapidated old Cushman motor scooter his father salvaged from somewhere. Sheets of roughly-snipped tin are loosely bolted to the rusted body wherever they will hold. He putts around the yard in circles, raising dust, and chases the squawking, flapping chickens, putting an end to any conversation. Martha scolds him in Spanish but it does little good. It's hard to talk with chickens in your hair.

When I leave the Corrillo's, Martha always walks me part way down the mountain, and her mother sends Felix, still clowning, to trail after us. When he isn't at home, her mother tells us we have to walk on opposite sides of an old fence that stretches down the mountain.

Martha is constantly and painfully on my mind. I hear her name in the rhythm of the wind that howls at night as I lie in bed, in the echo of the chapel bell that wakes me each morning.

"Oh, Bill, what are we going to do with you?" Father Bede asks. "You're lovable and affectionate and some old matron will be very unhappy if she doesn't get you. I've gotten to know some women myself, and I've fallen in love with their spiritual beauty. And when you get to know them this way, to want something physical is very natural. It's tough being a priest."

"No old matron, please, Father Bede," I say. "Just Martha. Martha is so gentle and unaffected; she doesn't pretend. Her eyes are beautiful. I'm getting to like her more than I wish I did."

"That's the best thing you've said, Bill. The Spanish girls like fair skin and brown hair. It's a novelty to them, something very different. If I talked to her father, he would probably let you marry her. He knows you could give her a better life than any of these poor Laro boys could. And she would make a loving, adoring wife. Martha would do everything she could to make you happy . . ."

"I'd want to make *her* happy."

"But you would probably have to live here in Laro, because Martha would never leave this area. Spanish families are very close-knit and tied to the land and their surroundings. And the young boys around here would be jealous and resentful. They would make it tough on you."

"I'm sure they would," I say. Then I tell him how the first time I met her, Martha snatched up little Karen, dusted off the chair, and offered it to me.

"That's the way these Spanish women are," Father Bede says. "One small gesture like that says more than you could say in a thousand words."

"The mountains skipped like rams, and the little hills like lambs" — *Psalm CXIV*

I never went to church at home; I didn't like it. But I like Mass here at the monastery, the way the brothers pray, in their black habits, chanting in the cold, dimly-lit stillness. It is no social bazaar with the smell of perfume, aftershave, and a minister calling more attention to himself than to God; it's just men praying quietly and intently for salvation. And there is no group-hugging and swooning to the strumming of a guitar: The "born-again" Christians haven't come along yet.

I always get up before dawn, while it is still dark and cold, to go to Mass. Occasionally there are a few of the Spanish people from Laro sitting in the pews.

I give thanks for good companionship, and for the friendship and kindness shown to me by men like Father Bede, Brother Frank, Brother Patrick, Deaf Don, and the others. I give thanks for the quiet and solitude, the start of a new day, and the happiness and contentment I now feel.

One morning when I go to Mass, still half asleep, I am startled to see a young Spanish girl sitting alone in an empty pew, and in an instant I am wide awake. She looks like Martha.

I sit down at the opposite end of the pew. She turns and smiles. It *is* Martha. Then she slides down next to me. We sit shoulder to shoulder, and she holds her missal between us so we can share it. Father Bede says Mass but I don't hear much of it.

After Mass I follow Martha outdoors. She looks beautiful in her long, black wool prayer shawl and blue cotton dress. The sun is up but a cold, porcelain moon still hangs in the sky.

I look around for Felix, but he is nowhere in sight. Martha seems to anticipate the question I might have asked.

"Felix ees not feeling so good. He ees home. Hees motor scooter heet a tree 'n' hees ankle ees tweested."

I ask how little Karen is, to change the subject.

"Karen ees not feeling so good either, Bill; she ate the clay you brought me."

"Hey, Martha, how's my favorite girl? It's great to see you!" It's Father Bede. "Hey, Bill, give Martha the tour. It's a nice morning for a walk."

I hesitate a moment for Martha's sake.

"Have you forgotten your vow of obedience?" he asks.

Martha laughs. "Come on, Bill!"

We hike down through the pasture behind the friary with Big Boy at our heels. The dry brush feels good underfoot.

"How ees Earlito?" Martha asks.

"I saw him yesterday. He had a toothache. Father Bede and I had to take him to the dentist in Ione. The other children begged to come along, seven was all we could pack into the back seat of my car, and the three of us in the front made ten. Earl still doesn't talk, but he whimpered a little; his tooth hurt. But he wanted me to sit there next to the dentist's chair. That made my day. I miss him. I'd like to see him a lot more often, the other kids, too, but I don't know how that could be worked out."

"Ee likes you, Bill," Martha says. "Felix and Karen like you, too. They even say they wish you were their older brother."

"They do? That's nice."

"Felix say to tell Father Bede he haff some more warms for him."

Father Bede offered to pay Felix a dime for every dozen worms he digs up and brings him. He wants Felix to feel included. Father Bede makes a little ceremony out of planting the worms in the worm garden by the porter's lodge, and that pleases Felix. The money from the sale of the worms to the trout fishermen is another project to aid the Spanish.

"Eet ees nice of Father Bede to do thees. Felix ees very proud. He haff a notebook 'n' he write down how many warms he sell 'n' how much monny he make."

I ask her how many worms Felix has sold to Father Bede.

"Hondreds."

"Are you and your sisters making lots of grottoes, Martha? Father Bede just sent a load in to Carlsbad in the bakery truck with One-eyed Ernie. He's found a dealer who will distribute them all over the state."

"The monny ees such a blessing," Martha says. "Eet helped pay for mother's medicine when she was sick. And we got papa's car running again, too."

"Father Bede has many ideas about starting some industries around here." Then I ask her if she needs more clay.

"I like eet when you comb to see me, Bill," she says. "But eet ees not necessary to breeng me clay or paper everytime, jus' comb anyway. Now maybe you comb more often. 'N' I haff plenty feathers. I tie so many trout flies I look like theese," she says, laughing, cocking her head, touching her nose and crossing her eyes.

"Is *that* how a trout looks?"

"No, that ees how *I* look. I will push you een the river sometime. Then you can see what a trout looks like."

"No more feathers," I promise. "Maybe I'll bring you cats instead, some of Brother Frank's dozens."

"Why does he haff so many cats, Bill?"

"How do you think we get our feathers?"

Martha laughs. "I will breeng *you* something, Bill. Tortillas. I make you some."

"I'd like that, Martha, very much."

Suddenly, Martha's hand is in mine. I can feel my pulse beating in the hand that holds her hand. The wind rustles the birds and the leaves chirp.

"I like you, Bill," Martha says.

"I like you, Martha, awfully much," I tell her.

"It's fun to be with you, Bill. You make me laugh."

"Knowing you is one of the nicest things that's ever happened to me."

We stop. Martha's hand is still in mine; I won't be the first one to let go. Martha is the most beautiful girl I have ever seen. She has lips that would melt in your mouth. In a second I would have kissed her, she's waiting, but just then we both look up to see Brother Patrick in his floppy cowboy hat loping through the field towards us.

"Oh no, what does he want?" Martha asks.

"Nuts, I don't know," I say. "I hope he wants to twist *his* ankle."

Martha laughs. "Oh, Bill, I haff to go now. Mother ees gone and Karen and Felix are home alone. We will see each other soon, no? I will miss you."

"I'll miss you, too," I say. "Even when I'm with you I miss you."

*If a bird wipes his beak on a rock on a mountain and
flies back once a year, when the mountain has
disappeared, that's an eternity*

On Sunday mornings after early Mass I often hike up the
mountain. The climb is steep and rocky.

Big Boy always tags along and I'm glad for his company. He will
bound ahead and disappear, and I'll whistle and shout, afraid he is lost.
Then he comes ripping out of the brush behind me, deliberately
scaring me out of my wits. "Don't worry about Big Boy," Brother
Vincent told me. "*He's* never lost. You don't know where he is, but he
knows where you are."

The mountainside is desolate and immense, stark dwarf-pine
and twisted piñon jutting here and there, boulders overhead as big as a
car. I always feel compelled to keep climbing, to go on and on, every
step another step further from the protection of the monastery, deeper
into the silence and mystery of the mountain.

I feel removed from all that is familiar, those things from which
one draws his self-identity: faces, friends, bed, and home.

Once a timber wolf the size of a deer skimmed by like a ghost, twenty feet away and going in the opposite direction, his feet touching the rocky ground so lightly they didn't make the slightest sound. Big Boy, who was right at my side, didn't even know it. He didn't see, smell, or hear him go by.

The climb is so steep that for stretches one has to crawl on hands and knees, and at the edge of the summit, twenty-five hundred feet up, it looks as though one could spit down on the roofs of the monastery buildings. The summit is a vast plateau of meadow, beautiful in the brilliant light, and beyond the meadow lies unfathomable wilderness.

One morning, halfway back down the mountain, I come unexpectedly upon a beat-up parked car that has driven up the fire trail. Inside it are half a dozen men, drinking, singing, and playing the guitar. Apprehensive, I hurry on by, but a little beyond, I hear a shrill whistle. "Hey, kid, come here," a voice yells.

I look over my shoulder. A young Spanish boy has gotten out of the car and is standing legs spread and hands on hips. His stance unsettles me, as if it is a taunt or a challenge.

I keep on walking, but he yells again, and I hesitate. My compulsion to see what he wants is as strong as my wariness and feeling of foreboding. Maybe they have car trouble, I think. Maybe he just wants to know what time it is. Maybe he wants matches.

Against my better judgment, I turn around and walk back.

"Hi, you don't have car trouble, I hope," I say as I reach him. "I can get to a telephone fast if you do."

"Hey man, come here, my brother says you pulled a knife on him at Alejandro's," he says in a hard voice.

He is short, thin, wiry.

Frightened and startled, I ask, "What are you talking about? I didn't do that."

"Oh yes you did, man, he says so. Are you calling my brother a liar?"

"That's crazy. I haven't been in Alejandro's, and I don't know your brother."

We stand close. My knees are shaking and feel like lead. His eyes are hard and opaque. One of the men in the car leans out and yells, "Leave the boy alone, you loco mono. Get back in the car."

"You one of them fat monks, eatin' lots of beefsteak? Fuck, man, you're not."

"I'm a friend of Father Bede's. I'm not a monk, but I'm staying at the monastery."

"Hey, I know who *you* are, man. You're a friend of the Corrillos, ain't you?"

"Yes, I know them."

"You stay away from Marta."

"Martha? Why should I?" I ask. "Martha's a friend of mine."

"Hey, she's my cousin, stay away from her you son-of-a-bitch."

"The hell I will, why should I stay away from her?"

"'Cause I say so. Let's go, chicken-shit."

He reaches out and insolently pulls on the zipper of my jacket. I slap his hand away, and a surge of adrenaline replaces my terror.

We grapple, roll on the ground, punching and clawing at each other. My glasses fly off.

Finally, I begin to gain an edge; I get him on his back and straddle him, trying to hold him down. I am amazed at his strength for the size he is, and I am running out of breath, black spots floating before my eyes. I am faintly aware that the men in the car are shouting at us.

Bucking and wriggling, he gets an arm loose and flails at me, cuffing me hard in the ear, raking my face with his fingernails trying to reach my eyes, and slaps me in the teeth with a backhand. Infuriated, spitting out blood, I move up on his chest, get a knee on his right arm near the shoulder, then I grab him by the hair with both hands and pummel his head up and down on the ground. I am aware that I am out of control; I somehow observe detachedly that what I am doing in my frenzy can not possibly result in anything but serious injury, perhaps even a broken neck.

"Had enough you bastard?" I shout, relaxing my hold.

"Let me up, man."

Still straddling him, I desperately pat the ground around me, trying to find my glasses. With a feeling of great relief, I find them, unbroken. Getting up, I put them on and a temple piece drops off. I bend over to pick it up. That is a mistake.

Suddenly, I'm on my back, frantically trying to raise myself up on my elbows but too weak to do so, nausea expanding in wider and wider circles, everything out of focus. For a long moment I struggle for consciousness, not knowing where I am or what has happened.

The spinning stops and I hear snarling and growling. Ten feet away the boy is on his back with Big Boy standing over him, ripping at his clothing.

"No, Big Boy, no, Big Boy, stop!" I shout. He looks up at me, the front of the Spanish boy's jacket hanging from his jaws. "Come here, Big Boy." Big Boy has ripped the front of his jacket and shirt off right to the flesh.

Wobbly, lightheaded, and full of rage I walk over to the Spanish boy. "You're a dirty fighter, you bastard. And that makes *you* the chicken-shit. You're a damn coward to hit me the way you did. Get up," I tell him, grabbing him by the arm.

"I'm not afraid of you, just your fuckin' dog. He'll chew me up."

"Big Boy chew *you* up? There's not a toothmark on you. Big Boy eats beefsteak, too, he'd gag on you."

I call to Big Boy and we start back down the mountain. Big Boy's teeth are chattering from the fray, and my legs are shaking. At the bottom, I sit down on the ground, shaken, my head aching, trying to figure things out before I go back to the monastery. I hate that boy in spite of what Father Bede has taught me about reaching out to others and loving them.

When I return to the friary it is noon, and the others have gathered to wait for Sunday dinner.

"My God, what happened to you?" Father Bede exclaims.

I tell him about my fight with the Spanish boy. "He said I pulled a knife on his brother at Alejandro's."

"That crazy punk. Are you all right, Bill? I don't like the way you look. I'm sorry all this had to happen."

"We used to have a problem with the young boys," Brother Vincent says. "They'd come in here at night and walk off with anything that wasn't nailed down. Big Boy put an end to that. Now they sit up in the hills and plink at our buildings with their .22s. We had Brother Thomas deputized. There's no law in Laro. Even the judge in Carlsbad is afraid to prosecute these kids; he's afraid they'll take revenge."

Brother Thomas says, "They can be brutal. They'll do anything. There was a boy in Laro who only had one eye, a bull had gouged out the other one. He was a nice kid, too. He was in love with a girl, she was in love with him, and they were going to get married. Another boy was jealous, he wanted her, too. So he got his friends together and they ganged up on the one-eyed boy, held him down on the ground so the kid who was jealous could kick out his good eye. He thought she wouldn't marry him if he was blind, but she did anyway. I had to help round up those kids. These buckles make good persuaders," Brother Thomas adds, tugging at the wide leather belt around the waist of his habit.

Brother Frank replies, sarcastically, "I'll bet you're real handy with that belt buckle. Better make sure your pants stay up."

"Oh, I know they're hot-blooded," Father Bede says, "But we have to pray for them, and offer them our love."

"And a tire-iron across the skull," Brother Frank adds.

Deeply troubled by my confrontation with the Spanish boy, I go to my room. The erratic heartbeat, which I had become conscious of as I came down the mountain after the fight, is still bothering me and I am worried. I am comfortable neither lying down nor sitting up, though I haven't told anyone about it. The trouble with my heart has happened before, but I don't ever remember it lasting this long.

Half an hour later when Father Bede comes to my room I tell him.

"Bill," he says, "one of the sisters in the convent is a nurse. Let's take your car and get over there quick."

Dr. Mason startles me with his discovery

At the convent the sister feels my pulse and listens to my heartbeat. Alarmed, she tells Father Bede to drive me to the hospital in Carlsbad and take me to the emergency room.

Father Bede drives seventy and eighty all the way; I'm afraid it's putting a strain on my old car as well as my heart.

At the hospital I am given an EKG, questioned and admitted. I urge Father Bede to go back to the monastery and get some sleep, but he says he won't leave until he gets the doctor's report. An attendant wheels me upstairs.

The doctor examines me. Then he asks if I know what has brought on the arrythmia. I tell him, "I got into a violent fight with a kid and afterwards the palpitations began."

"Have you ever had this problem before?"

I tell him it has happened three times to my knowledge. He

asks me what brought it on, and I answer, "I was extremely angry on all of these occasions, so angry I had to gasp for breath. When I get this angry it literally feels as if it's going to explode right up through my head."

"That's a neurological sensation," he replies. "I'm going to order some tests for you. And I'll want to know more about your history."

"How long do you think I'll have to be here?"

"I can't answer that question at the moment. If your arrhythmia doesn't subside spontaneously in a day or two, I'll prescribe a drug for you that will correct it."

"The only way I can describe the sensation is that it feels as if my heart has jumped the track, so to speak."

"Well," Father Bede says, "I'm glad to know you're in good hands. I'll be in touch, and the doctor has my number. I'll say a special prayer for you."

Exhausted, I try to sleep, but just as I doze off, the old man in the next bed calls out shrilly, "The coast of Maine is clear, the coast of Maine is clear," apparently hallucinating, and I'm wide awake.

I just get back to sleep, and once more I'm awakened: "Feed your dogs here, feed your dogs here, feed your dogs here."

That finally brings the nurse: "Who's got dogs to feed? Hush up. You're disturbing the other patients."

"Have a free tilkin, want a tilkin, here, take one, they're free."

"What's a 'tilkin,' Mr. Geiger?" she asks.

"Have a free tilkin, have a free tilkin, have a free tilkin," he chants.

This goes on most of the night.

By the morning of my third day, after tests and observation, the cardiologist comes by and asks me how I feel.

"I feel fine," I tell him. "Last night before I went to bed, the nice old gentleman over there, my roommate, asked me if I would help him get out of his chair and into bed. I had to lift him, and he was heavier than I thought. But immediately afterwards, the arrhythmia was gone, I don't know why. But I feel fine."

The cardiologist smiles. "Sometimes one kindness returns another. Occasionally a sudden, strenuous exertion like that will restore normal heartbeat, but we don't recommend it."

He listens to my heart. "Sounds good. I want to keep you one more day though."

"Fine," I tell him. "I've been wondering, is there any chance I could talk to a psychologist or psychiatrist while I'm here?"

"Do you want to talk about these spells of anger you have that you think are linked to your arrhythmia? I think that can be arranged, perhaps as early as this afternoon."

The fight has stirred up my problems once again, the same problems I had when I came to the monastery, the same problems I will have to face again, when and if the day comes that I will have to leave the protection and peace of the monastery. I write a note and ask the nurse if she will put it in my file for the psychiatrist:

"Behind the exterior of a meek, frightened person almost totally unable to assert himself, which makes him feel completely at the mercy of others, is anger, frustration, destructiveness, and self-loathing. I have felt this way for many years. I don't like to hurt anyone's feelings, be unkind, or hurt anyone physically; I can't stand to see people mistreated. But I have a problem with anger that scares me. Most of the time I'm passive with people, keeping my distance for safety. But before I happened to end up at the monastery, where I am now, I was at the end of my rope, feeling that I could no longer take care of myself in terms of a job, food, a place to live, that I was completely helpless, that I could no longer contain the anger and turmoil inside, that I was on the verge of exploding, possibly causing great injury, maybe even killing someone, or killing myself. I would like to have some help with my problems."

Later that afternoon Dr. Mason, in his mid-fifties, gentle and soft-spoken, arrives at my bedside. I am wary and apprehensive, because of my experiences with doctors and psychiatrists I had seen earlier. I am afraid that he, too, might be unsympathetic.

Dr. Mason introduces himself and says, "I understand you're here because of some problems with your heart, but the reports show that it's nothing to be too much alarmed about."

"Yes, I feel okay. I wrote down some things that I'd like to talk to you about."

"I've read your note, Bill. It tells me a lot, but I'd like you to fill me in on some details. You have some problems that you've apparently suffered from most of your life and have never found help for."

I begin to think that I'm going to like Dr. Mason.

"Well," I tell him, "they showed up early, particularly when I started school and tried to learn how to read and write. No matter how hard I tried, I couldn't catch on. I'd get more and more flustered. I felt bewildered and lost, struggling like a fly stuck to a streamer of flypaper. The other kids ridiculed me and some of the teachers did, too, when I so often couldn't answer questions or follow simple directions. I can't remember when I wasn't in terror of the classroom, the other students, the teacher. I was the butt of schoolyard cruelty, a ten-cent package of Kool-Aid powder shaken up my nostrils while I was held on the ground by three boys: 'Now you won't be so empty headed,' they said. I nearly suffocated."

I tell him of my feelings from the early grades that I am and always will be a failure, how I became passive with other people and fearful of them, while angry at myself. "I've always had the feeling that in some way I'm retarded or that there's a short circuit somewhere in my brain."

"This may indeed be a neurological problem," Dr. Mason says. "I think you may have dyslexia. I'd like you to take some tests."

"I've never heard of it," I say, startled. "What is it?"

"From what you've told me, I'd guess you've had a long history of mishandling anger and frustration. And you've accumulated some emotional scars from your difficult relationships with others since childhood. I believe your problems stem from a learning disability that in your case wasn't recognized early enough. To answer your question, dyslexia is a neurological disorder centered in the brain. The dyslexic child has severe difficulties when it comes to language skills, especially reading and writing, as you say you did."

"I always felt completely cut off and separate from the rest of the class. I felt dazed and dense."

"Yes, you would've felt that way. Dyslexia is an inability to recognize words, to spell, or to understand what you read, sometimes compounded by other problems, such as poor coordination."

"I certainly had a hard time," I say. "I got farther and farther behind the others in my class. My mother and father would drill me over and over, but I could not retain anything I read, and couldn't memorize anything either. I remember how I dreaded being called on to read aloud, because I read so poorly, and because the others laughed when I read words wrong, like 'nam,' or 'dab,' or 'tac,' instead of man, bad, or cat."

"We call that reverse or mirror-reading," Dr. Mason explains. "It's a fairly frequent symptom of dyslexia."

"My twin brother and the other children seemed to catch on to arithmetic, spelling, and reading without much trouble, and the teachers didn't understand why I couldn't."

"Yes," Dr. Mason says, "school administrators and teachers for a long time didn't recognize the signs of dyslexia. Unlike his classmates who can soak up what they're taught and then give it back in class, the dyslexic is confused, he can't hand it back, he gets tangled up, he has problems in sorting things out, he lacks order."

Suddenly, Mr. Geiger, my roommate, interrupts us. He is 'preaching' again: "Jesus Christ and His twelve bald testicles . . .!" he calls out loudly.

Dr. Mason laughs, but continues, "Because of his failure to keep up, combined with snickers from his classmates or a humiliating response from his teacher, the dyslexic becomes convinced that he's dumb."

"In fifth grade," I tell him, "I had an arithmetic teacher who would become furious with me when I couldn't catch on. She'd grab me by the shoulders and shake me so hard that once my glasses flew off. I was frightened to death of her. I'd wet my pants when she shook me."

"That's an awful experience for a child to go through," Dr. Mason says.

"Earlier you mentioned that poor coordination could be a problem for a dyslexic," I tell him. "I was so poorly coordinated that grade and high school team captains never chose me and I had to be assigned by the teacher to a team, with groans from the team members who were stuck with me."

"And so the defeats and their effects accumulated," he adds.

"In high school and the beginning of college, memorizing and organizing were almost impossible tasks for me and still are. I'd work like hell, but when I faced an exam, I'd just draw a blank. I'd become furious at myself. Even when the teacher was lecturing, I couldn't keep up.

"And in my despair, I'd exult in my failure, partly to punish my parents who warned me years ago that I'd be sorry someday if I didn't study hard enough, and partly to prove to them that I was as dumb as they thought I was."

"That's sad," Dr. Mason says. "It's shocking that as recently as a dozen years ago, a dyslexic was often thought to be retarded or brain-damaged. We now know that that's not true. Now, are you ready to take . . ."

"Oh, my God!" I say. Mr. Geiger has gotten out of bed and is standing there tottering. I run over to him. "He's not supposed to get out of bed."

"Did you ever see a man shit standing up?" he asks, lifting his

117

hospital gown and proceeding to demonstrate. Old age and decay have stripped him of his freedoms and now he's rebelling. Hurriedly, I ring for the nurse while I steady him.

Ignoring the confusion, Dr. Mason continues. "Are you ready to take those tests I mentioned?"

"I look forward to that," I tell him, "and I'm grateful to you. If I am dyslexic, I think it will be good to know that there are reasons for my failures."

The next morning the learning-disability specialist, Dr. Berns, comes to my room. She begins with a flash card test. She holds up a card with four objects on it, a tree, a cat, a house, a baseball mitt. I can take as much time as I want to memorize the objects and their sequence; then, putting the card down, she asks me what's on it. I get more and more rattled and frustrated as she shows each card, some twenty-five of them. Sometimes I can only remember one object, never a sequence.

Then she gives me a booklet with several sections of different kinds of tests in it, asks me to fill in the answers, and leaves it with me.

I start on the first section, a numbers-progression test, the kind of thing I had done before in school and college, and on which I've always scored very low. I do poorly on it, and it makes me furious.

A vocabulary test makes me feel a little more confident, and interpreting a list of proverbs begins to interest me: "When the cat's away, the mice will play." "Sure they will," I write. "They don't want their noses pressed to the mainstream grindstone; they'd rather explore," and for "Don't count your eggs before they hatch," I answer, "That's right, you might find twins."

Drawing a male and a female figure, not omitting eyes, nose, mouth, ears, hands, and feet, comes next.

The second half of the booklet is entirely made up of a great variety of questions needing subjective answers, such as "A woman's role in marriage is . . .?" "Would you rather be a leader or a follower?" "Neither."

I finish by noon and start in on another booklet, a "Multi-Phasic Personality Inventory" test.

Dr. Mason stops by later that afternoon. "Dr. Berns and I have gone over your tests, and the results, along with the discussions you and I have had, make it quite clear that you are dyslexic. In each section of the test, you either scored as high as you can go, or you hit bottom; these extremes are common in dyslexia. On the numbers-progression, you hit bottom. On the vocabulary test you did very well. By the way, I enjoyed your drawings, especially the little old lady, but you thought you'd fool me, putting woman's clothing on the man, didn't you? He's actually wearing a monk's habit, isn't he?"

"I thought I could trick you. But the little old lady is my seven-year-old niece. I don't draw very well."

"Sure you do. You did bomb out on the flash cards. Poor memory and lack of retention are problems, I'd gather, in your struggle with class work, where you have to read texts and remember what you read."

"That's right."

"You have another difficulty. In discussions with me and others here your thinking often seems a little fuzzy-headed. You speak hesitantly, as if groping for a thought and the words to express it, another problem dyslexics frequently have."

"That's true," I tell him. "Earlier, when I went to parties, friends would sometimes impersonate me, stumbling in their speech, to amuse the others."

"Humiliation, as well as failure, is something dyslexics . . ."

"Hey, two-legged mule, my urinal wants your nose stuck in it," shouts Mr. Geiger.

"He wants what?" Dr. Mason asks.

"He wants me to empty his urinal. He likes me to wait on him, toothbrush, glass of water, extra blanket, and so on." Whispering, I tell Dr. Mason, "He calls me 'My guardian angel, my Hercules, my finest possession,' and tells me I'm to be 'highly reprimanded.' The other day he told me how he was invited to a dinner party, sat down, absentmindedly removed his false teeth and dropped them in his water glass. Sorry for interrupting, Doctor," I say.

"Well, as I was saying, people have so often been ignorant of the problems dyslexics face, and can be cruel and thoughtless. But I want to tell you that in the subjective-answer section of the test, you did well. Your answers were clear and concise. A dyslexic will often do very well in some areas, very poorly in others, because his skills are often mixed, sometimes to quite a degree."

"I did poorly in *all* areas. If it's true that I'm dyslexic, how can I get over it? What causes it in the first place?"

"The causes aren't really understood," he tells me. "There are many theories. I tend to go along with the idea that in the majority of cases dyslexia is inherited, that it's not a defect or brain damage. Few of those suffering from it ever outgrow it. Many do, however, find ways of coping with it.

"You have, to some extent, although you may not realize it. That note you wrote me, explaining your problems, shows you are able to express your thoughts in writing clearly enough."

"I worked for over an hour on that brief note."

"You may never excel in reading," he continues, "but the system you've devised, of outlining each chapter of a book, then reading and re-reading as you go, will be of great help in understanding and retaining what you read."

"I'm reading *The Confessions Of St. Augustine*, a gift from Father Bede, and greatly enjoying it. I think it's the first book I've read outside the classroom. I hated reading."

"Too, you are compensating for your earlier lack of coordination by the regular program of exercise that you've told me you have followed for several years.

"They should have identified you in school, or earlier, so that you could have been given special teaching. This is terribly important for dyslexics."

"I remember," I tell him, "the grade school supervisor who told my parents I was retarded after I scored low in an early-grade group test. I suppose I could've been put in a school for the retarded, and maybe ended up in a mental institution with the emotional problems I developed?"

"Yes. Because the reasons for your language difficulties weren't recognized soon enough, over the years you've developed the problems one might expect. We'll talk about these problems tomorrow, when we'll look at your personality-inventory results."

I spend much of the night going over the discussions Dr. Mason and I have had about dyslexia.

The next morning Dr. Mason comes around with the results of the PI, interpreted by a psychologist, which he reads to me:

"Bill shows a notable distress reaction with considerable components of depression, anxiety, tension, withdrawal, and diminished functioning. Bill is inclined toward internalizing. He works from a perfectionist framework with high expectations that continually frustrate him; this demanding style may in part be an effort to control his anger. He is very uncomfortable letting others get close to him."

"I do avoid people out of fear and mistrust. In the monastery, though," I tell him, "I've made some good friends, Father Bede, Brother Frank, and Brother Patrick, too. I know Father Bede has helped many others, and he has helped me. I like it at the monastery. I might even stay on, I've been thinking about it a great deal lately."

"Okay, Bill," he says. "But there are some deep-rooted problems that I want to get at. We're just beginning to see the emotional price dyslexics have paid through their years of struggling, always experiencing failure, influenced by the reactions they receive from others, and . . ."

"Bill, Bill, Bill." It's Mr. Geiger. "Do you see those Hungarian sausages floating around up there?" he asks.

"Yes, sure I do," I tell him, not wanting him to think he is nuts.

"You do?" he exclaims. "Then you must be as crazy as I am."

Dr. Mason frowns, I smile. "It's a relief to find out there's a reason for my past failures, but I don't think I can get rid of these angry feelings I have toward myself and others."

"Gradually I hope you'll let down some of these protective barriers you have and learn how to relate better to others. Your life has been a lonely one because you've shut yourself off from others."

"I have friends," I tell him. "At the monastery."

"We have a 'Feelings Group' here at the hospital. In the right situation it seems you respond to warmth with warmth. Letting others get to know you is important. And in our Feelings Group you'd be in a safe environment where you could risk letting down some of your barriers and exposing how you feel to others."

His proposal that I join a Feelings Group frightens me. With his diagnosis of dyslexia, I had been feeling that I was on my way to understanding my problems and getting help. But my hopes plummet; joining a Feelings Group is an utter impossibility. I am unable to expose my thoughts and feelings to an individual, let alone a group, after years of terror and apprehension, attack and ridicule in the classroom and on the playground.

"How many days a week would it be?" I ask, shaken, feigning an interest. "A day or two?"

"I'm afraid a day or two a week wouldn't be enough. You need the intensive help you could get here as a patient in the hospital."

I ask him how long I'd have to stay.

"A month, maybe longer. You've had these problems for a long time. You'd attend our Feelings Group, get some counseling, and probably some medication. You'd live in close proximity to the other patients, some of whom you might not like; you'd have to find a way to cope with these pressures without running away. On the other hand, you'd very likely meet patients with whom you could relate, and we'd hope that some of your barriers would begin to fall away."

"I appreciate what you've done for me," I tell him. "But I already know people I can relate to. My friends at the monastery. I want to go back."

Dr. Mason frowns. "It's too easy putting off unpleasant things that we want to avoid. If you don't get tough with yourself and say, 'I need help now and I'm going to get it,' you may never get the help you need."

"I'm getting a lot of help from Father Bede."

"Part of becoming mature is accepting responsibility. That means supporting yourself."

"Are you talking about the monastery?" I ask, angry. "I earn my keep."

"Have you found escape from the world at this monastery of yours, where you can avoid facing your problems, and avoid making your own decisions?"

"How would you know what this experience at the monastery is doing for me?" I ask. "I hate what you seem to think are my reasons for being there. I've gotten more help there than you'd ever know. I was at the end of my rope, something bad would've happened. 'P' for perish, that's what it would've been, the end; then I came to the monastery and met Father Bede."

"Well, Bill . . ."

"I don't want to talk any more," I tell him.

"Your cardiologist has released you, you're free to go. If you decide you need help, you know where to reach me."

"That's not very likely." I grab my suitcase, already packed, brush by him, and nod to old Mr. Geiger on the way out. "The coast of Maine is clear!" he calls out, saluting me. At ninety-six, he still wants to drink, dance, chase girls, and asked me to go halves with him on a canoe.

Father Bede comes to pick me up. In his usual high spirits, he says, "It's sure good to see you, buddy. It'll be great to have you back.

So how are you? What's the diagnosis? The prognosis?"

"Heart's okay, but it's pining for Martha," I reply. I decide not to tell him about dyslexia or the Feelings Group.

He laughs. "Martha's going to get you yet, Bill! She's been asking about you."

"She has?" I ask excitedly.

"I told her you were in the hospital for some tests. She's concerned about you. She stopped by several times."

"Really?" My face burns.

When we get back to the monastery, everyone seems glad to see me and wants to know about my stay in the hospital.

"They feed dogs and hand out free tilkins," I say, then explaining about my roommate.

When we are alone I tell Brother Frank, "I sure missed being here. I hope you haven't had any trouble because of my experience in the mountains."

"No, we haven't. And don't let that Laro kid scare you away from Martha. Some young punk from around here will get his hands on her, and she'll have ten kids and have gone to seed before you know it. You'll never find another girl like her. You should be making love to her. Of course you'd have to marry her first. Father Bede has offered to talk to her father."

"She wants to be an artist, Frank," I reply. "I don't think she'll have a dozen kids and go to seed. She's bright, kind, and gentle."

Back in my room, I agonize over what to do. Shall I tell Martha about the fight, or would it be better if I just stay away?

Tha painful memories of days and nights, years of longing for a girl, taunt me. Martha is not a daydream or a fantasy. Could I take care of her; am I ready if she is willing, to settle down to a job to pay for furniture and babies?

She probably would never be willing to leave her world, Father

Bede had told me, and I would never be accepted in hers. But "A treasure like Martha is worth fighting for," he'd said that, too.

I know it is better to stay away, but I ache for Martha, heart, lung, and guts, and I know I can't stay away.

*The beauty of a bleak and desolate winter afternoon
makes one yearn to be close to others and want them to
be close to him*

It is good to be back at the monastery. I like the high-ceilinged refectory on the second floor, large and sparely furnished, the starkness and brightness of its bare walls, and tall curtainless windows overlooking the valley, the long table covered with a yellowed and threadbare oilcloth, the wooden napkin ring and linen napkin at each place setting.

But my favorite room is the large friary with beams as big around as a man's waist, small bulbs in a row on top of each beam covered with lampshades snipped out of tin and decorated with patterns made by punching holes, typically Spanish. I like the big stone fireplace and the smell of a piñon fire, the large double doors with glass panes on either side of it that look out on the grassy or snowfilled courtyard, the cloister and the monk's cells.

I like it when Frank, coming in from the courtyard, opens the door and characteristically kicks the sill to knock the snow off his shoes.

It is a bleak, gray day, two months to the day since I came to the monastery. There is no work on Saturday afternoon. Father Bede, Brother Patrick, Deaf Don, Frank and I are sitting in the friary. The wind moans and howls and the steam jets hiss softly and the pipes thump. The fire in the fireplace burns low. Each man sits alone, lost in his private thoughts. Brother Patrick puffs on his pipe. Is he thinking about and missing his mother back in Ireland? And Father Bede, is he remembering the girl he once told me about that he loved and lost? His love for her, he had said, was as strong then as his love for Christ is now. Deaf Don, lost in his silent world, what is he thinking? And Frank, is he daydreaming about the fun and camaraderie of a Saturday afternoon in a Denver bar with his friends?

At this moment I feel the intense aloneness of each man, in spite of their being united in a sense of community and their day to day endeavors and activities, and I feel a bittersweet sadness and longing akin to the incessant howling of the wind and the weather outside. I realize that I can never fully know each one—nor they me—nor even know very much about the mystery of their lives.

Evening, and Brother Patrick, who has eaten earlier, entertains us at the dinner table by reading from a secular book while the rest of us eat. Brother Patrick is the most popular choice as reader because of his heavy broque and his dramatic inflections and the arching of his eyebrows. Besides, the others don't like to read at the table, they want to eat. He is reading from *Saints Among The Savages*, and when he comes to the place where the French priest bids a tearful farewell to a dear friend, Brother Patrick hesitates at a common French word.

"Ah-dee-o," he tries, and shakes his head. "Odd-e-ou? Ah-dee-a? Ah-day?"

The others, who have stopped eating, sit in silence.

"Ah-doe? Ah-die-o? Oh, hell," he says finally, "GOOD-BYE!"

After dinner we gather in the recreation room in the basement. Brothers Vincent and Frank, Father Burkhart and I play hearts.

Father Bede sits by himself, as usual, at a card table at the back of the room, glueing small crosses to hunks of petrified wood we found in the desert. 'Father Bird and his religious junk,' Brother Frank calls it.

Brother Patrick marches in with a basket of clothes for Father Alfonse to iron and sets up the ironing board for him.

Brother Thomas leans back in his chair, his engineer boots propped against the wall, listening to a country-western record, Roy Orbison's plaintive wail, on his dime-store record player.

Brother Patrick leaves the recreation room for several minutes and comes back with a cardboard box, which he unobtrusively sets on the table, and then sits down.

Brother Frank looks up: "Candy for the children of Laro!" he shouts, jumping up.

There is a scramble for the box. "Hands off the licorice until I get my share," Father Burkhart warns.

Brother Frank grabs a handful of Hershey Bars. Brother Thomas drops a handful of cellophane-wrapped candies over his shoulder into his cowl. Brother Patrick, in silent disapproval, won't touch the candy.

"There are some nice old ladies who drive all the way from Roswell once or twice a month just to leave this stuff for Father Bede to take to Laro when he says Mass," Brother Frank explains to me. " 'Candy for the children of Laro,' they always say. Somehow it never gets there."

Father Alfonse, ironing done, his pants cuffs still safety-pinned mid-shin and flashlight in his lap, hums softly, content as a mother hen in his care for us. He rocks slowly in his rocking chair and snaps his fingers out of time to Hank Snow's "Gambler's Guitar."

Evening recreation ends and Brother Patrick tugs the knotted end of the bell rope that hangs down through the ceiling like the tail of a lion. The bell's wooden supports atop the roof whine and groan. We climb the spiral staircase and black-cowled shadows glide through the dark friary to the chapel. For fifteen minutes low voices chorus Hail Marys in the cold stillness, and finally: "As-it-was-in-the-beginning-is-now-and-ever-shall-be, world-without-end, a-men. May-God-be-with-you." Then there is a shuffle of feet, the light is turned out, and the cell doors in the courtyard slam. Day has ended.

Big Boy is asleep outside on an old couch by the friary entrance, whimpering and growling in his dog dreams. His black snoot is covered with scar tissue from an encounter with a bobcat.

I whistle softly to wake him and he jumps down to follow me to my room. There are no city lights to soften the night sky and the heavens are deep, vast, and brilliant.

The only sounds are Big Boy's even breathing and the low hiss of the gas heater. Large white shapes, luminous in the starlight, glide by my window. I hear them brush against the building, and the hollow ring of small iron bells. The cows have come up from the pasture to supper on the grass in the yard. Big Boy awakens, growls, noses his way out the door, and heavy hooves pound the ground as he scatters them.

The night is dark and cold and absolutely still. I fall asleep, content.

A monastic life is much more than an escape from the world and the harshness of life

The next morning when we are mixing plaster to do some repairs around the windows in the refectory, Brother Patrick says, "Bill, I'ave a feelin', I do, t'at ya get a wee bit lonely sittin' back t'ere in the laity all by yourself, 'n' not bein' able to join in with the rest of us."

"I do," I say, "but Deaf Don is usually there and we sit together."

"Father Bede would like ta give ya a rosary, 'e would, but only if ya want it, t'at is, so ya can join with us, like Deaf Don does, in prayin' ta the Blessed Mother at Complin."

"I would like one," I tell him, very much pleased.

We go to the friary and I pick out one with wooden beads. "Take the one with the glass beads, Bill, it costs more," he urges, but I keep the one I have.

"You'll be safe with t'at wherever ya travel, Bill, even if yer on a plane. Father Bede will be wantin' ta bless it for ya."

Then he goes to his cell and comes back with a small card with a picture of Christ on the front, and on the back it says, 'Brother Patrick O'Grady, Perpetual Profession of Vows, May 3, 1952,' which he offers to me shyly.

"I'll treasure it," I tell him, and run over to my room to put it in a safe place.

I ask Brother Patrick how one actually goes about becoming a Catholic.

"Ah, friend, I t'ought you'd be askin' t'at question one of these days!" he says. "Did ya know we get a two-week vacation every five years, 'n' can fly, free, anywhere in the world we want to?"

That night Father Bede comes to my room. "Brother Patrick says you want to become a Catholic," he says.

"I was just asking questions," I reply.

"I thought so. Brother Patrick gets a little overly enthusiastic sometimes. He had you converted, baptized, and ready to take your perpetual vows. You haven't been here long enough to know much about our faith. On the other hand, I thought you might have been attracted by the beauty you see in our lives here. Sometimes that is enough."

"Bill, I would like to have you quit floating and drifting. I love and trust you, and I want you to realize that others need you more than you know. I want you to find some purpose in your life."

"I don't want to be a drifter either. And I admire and trust you more than anyone I know."

"No, Bill, it is not from me that the power comes to give light and meaning to your life," he says sharply. "We have to help ourselves, and do the best we can, but we need God's help, we can't do it alone."

When he leaves, I listen to his footsteps echo down the hall and the front door slam. Then silence. Father Bede's words have shaken me. I feel a kind of rejection in them. Have I been leaning on him too much? Is he trying to put some distance between us? Father Bede, Brothers Frank and Patrick are the kind of friends I've never had before. I admire each of them, partly because they contrast so sharply with my own sense of self. In their lives I sense an inner freedom, the right to be themselves, to do and say what they like, each one behaving in his own way.

"As monks, we strive for selflessness," Father Bede has said. "That's forgetting about yourself, and until you can do this, you can't really love others, and you can't really love God."

I realize that I myself, with my buried hatreds and angers, and suspicions of others, have a long way to go before I can love in the Christian sense.

I'm happy at the monastery, with the privacy and solitude, the simplicity of life. I feel ready to reject a world obsessed with money, in which people are unkind, uncaring, and often unbelievably cruel towards each other.

But I realize, when Father Bede talks about all power on heaven and earth coming from God and that we can do nothing by ourselves, that a monastical life is more than a rejection of the world or an escape to quiet and solitude. In its vows of poverty, obedience, stability, and chastity, it demands a total surrender and dedication to the spiritual that I do not know how to make.

Thanksgiving, loaded with memories, is a time of longing, sadness, and joy

The weather turns warm, and it begins to rain. It pours steadily for three days, a solid, driving rain, and just as I think it is raining as hard as it can, it rains harder.

Brother Patrick and I are stuck with indoor jobs. "We'll mop and wax the floor here in the friary," he says, after lunch the third day. "I'll meet you here at one o'clock. Ah, Bill, scrubbin' 'n' polishin', t'ats for the sisters down in the convent."

I stretch out on the deacon's bench in front of the fire, where I sometimes rest at noon. I'm drowsy and I could easily fall asleep, but in a kind of daydream, I hear a loud explosion. The piñon logs crackle, the radiator hisses, the rain pelts the windows, and the odd feeling that something is about to happen persists; finally I force myself to get up and drag myself over to my room.

I lie in bed thinking that the others would think I was crazy if I told them, "Don't go into the friary this afternoon, it's not safe."

Just as I am falling asleep, Brother Patrick bursts in. "Did ya 'ear it?" he asks.

"Hear what? I've been dozing."

"Father Bede and I were up in the kitchen, and we t'aught the boiler 'ad exploded. Come 'n' 'ave a look, Bill!"

I follow him to the friary on the run.

The rain had collected on the flat roof rimmed by a wall. It seeped through, cracking and loosening the thick adobe ceiling, and the entire ceiling collapsed.

We stand there, Father Bede, Brother Frank, Brother Patrick and I, looking at the large blocks of adobe, tons of it, spread over every walking step of the floor from one end of the room to the other. The deacon's bench itself is covered with adobe chunks.

Hesitantly, I tell them about my daydream.

"You could've been killed, Bill," Brother Patrick says.

"Thank God for your divine premonition," Father Bede adds. "God has special plans for you. 'They have ears that do not hear, eyes that do not see.' Be careful, Bill, don't miss your mark."

"Yeah, better line up your sights and get a good Bede on it," Brother Frank says, laughing.

We do not usually have dessert, but that night, as a special treat, Deaf Don serves us chocolate ice cream.

"I asked the milkman to drop it off," Father Burkhart explains, "to celebrate Bill's narrow escape. Damn stuff's expensive, too!"

When I awake the next morning, Thanksgiving day, a soft snow has fallen during the night.

I go to the friary to wait for breakfast. Everyone has gathered. We follow each other upstairs to the refectory, and Brother Thomas carries a ladder. There is a trap door in the ceiling and we climb out onto the flat roof.

A stark, unbroken whiteness covers the valley. It is silent and still, nothing moves, and even a black horse down in the pasture stands motionless. The sky is overcast, low and luminous, and it is difficult to tell where the valley ends and the sky begins. Colors are vividly intense. The barn looks very red, the lone cottonwood in the middle of the pasture very black, its branches zigzagging upward at sharp angles against the whiteness like cracks in an egg shell.

It is chilly and the brothers pull up their black hoods. We stand there for minutes and no one speaks. Father Burkhart crosses himself and so do the others. Then we file down silently to breakfast.

After a quiet day of prayer and rest, we gather for our turkey dinner. The table, lit by candlelight, is covered with a linen cloth. Deaf Don has put a small pleated paper cup of jelly beans and candy corn at each setting.

I have never spent a Thanksgiving away from home, and I suffer a sharp pang of homesickness for the faces around our family table; the funny turkey cutouts my younger brother made for each of us; the extra sliver of pumpkin pie for the one who was brave enough to eat the turkey neck; the little boiled onions, and our giggles when jabbing them with a fork made the insides telescope out halfway across the plate; and after dinner, getting up and marching around the table, led by my younger brother, who had originated the custom, to kiss my mother and father for the good dinner.

Perhaps my mother, father, and brothers are sitting down for their Thanksgiving dinner a thousand miles away at the very instant we are. I can see the old house at the top of the steep hill, sitting high above the flat surrounding countryside with the view from the tall dining room windows of vast snowy Iowa fields of corn stubble and frozen plowed earth stretching all the way to the western horizon.

The beautiful face of a young woman brings me back to the present; she and her husband, friends of Father Burkhart, have joined us at the table.

Father Burkhart is clean-shaven for once and wearing a clean habit, buttoned to the neck and unspotted with toothpaste or food stains.

Brother Patrick appears wearing a frilly white bib apron, which he must have dug out of the old clothes in the barn, over his black habit. His tousled black hair looks as if it had been combed with a scrub brush.

"Don't look at him," Brother Frank tells me, "he's just trying to attract attention in that get-up."

Brother Patrick pours red wine into thin-stemmed crystal glasses.

When I tell Brother Patrick I don't care for any, Brother Frank nudges me. "What, you don't drink wine?" he whispers. "Let him pour it in your glass. I'll drink it for you."

Deaf Don serves the turkey. Brother Patrick helps him bring in the big bowls of mashed potatoes and vegetables.

Father Burkhart prays loudly and clearly without gazing out the window or reaching for food, and crosses himself slowly and deliberately. Father Bede offers prayer, too: "Oh bless us, Father, Son, and Holy Spirit. Put the Devil out, and Bill in."

I am surprised and pleased.

The wine disappears quickly, and Brother Patrick opens a second bottle. Father Burkhart gulps his down half a glass at a time, and puts his elbow in the creamed corn.

"This reminds me," he says, "of the woman who goes to the market to buy a Thanksgiving turkey. 'This one's too small,' she tells the butcher. 'This one's too big.' 'This one costs too much.' Finally the butcher gets impatient and he turns to the lady and says, 'Lady, you don't need a turkey. What you need is a goose!' " Father Burkhart's hand shoots up in the air with the middle finger extended.

No one laughs except Father Burkhart and Brother Frank. I laugh inside. The young couple stare down at their plates. But Father Burkhart wipes his eyes, blows his nose in his linen table napkin, and repeats the punch line.

"Take my wine glass out to the kitchen and refill it," Frank whispers. "And the level you fill it to measures the amount of faith I have in you." I bring it back filled to the brim.

I try to keep my eyes on my plate, but Brother Frank gapes at the beautiful young woman without embarrassment. Father Burkhart scowls at him.

"Where are you folks from?" Brother Frank asks her, and she says Florida.

"I hitchhiked through your state once," he says. Then he asks her if she knows the Bible story about the lost coin: " 'What woman, having ten drachmas, if she loses one drachma, does not light a lamp and search carefully until she finds it.' "

Brother Frank continues. "I spent the night in some jerkwater town. The county was 'dry' and there wasn't a damn thing to do. A group of Jehovah's Witnesses were holding a tent revival. I was with some friends and we decided to go in.

"A fat kid, about fifteen, with a shrill, whiny voice was giving a long drawn-out account of the parable of the lost silver piece.

"Finally I couldn't take it anymore. I walked up the aisle to the front, I had a fifty-cent piece in my pocket, and I flipped it at him. 'Here's your stinking coin,' I told him."

"Oh my, what happened then?" she asks.

"They picked me up and threw me out on my ass!" Brother Frank pauses. " 'Ear,' I should've said."

After dinner I hear Brother Frank tell Deaf Don he'll stay and help with the dishes.

"We don't need help, t'anks," Brother Patrick tells him.

"You're getting it anyway," Brother Frank answers sharply. "I'll take over. You go to recreation, Patrick."

"That's the first time Frank's offered to help in the kitchen," I hear Brother Vincent tell Father Burkhart.

"Why the sudden change?" Father Burkhart asks.

"He wants to drink up the wine we didn't finish."

We go down to evening recreation. Father Burkhart, Brothers

Vincent and Thomas, and I play hearts. Father Alfonse rocks slowly as he darns a pair of socks. Brother Patrick sits by himself, reading his missal.

Brother Frank is still up in the kitchen finishing off the dishes and the wine. When he walks in half an hour later, we all look up apprehensively. He strolls over to the record player. We are all listening to Hank Williams: "I wandered so aimless, life filled with sin, I wouldn't let my dear Saviour in . . ." Without asking, Brother Frank lifts the needle, takes the record off, puts on a lively Irish jig, and turns the sound up. Then he jerks a chair up against Brother Patrick's and sits down.

"That's what I call good music," he says loudly. Brother Patrick nods.

"Good Irish music, isn't it, Patrick?" he continues. Brother Patrick nods again.

"Hey, Patrick, I could listen to that all night," he says, nudging him. Brother Patrick shrugs, re-lights his pipe, and goes on reading.

"When I was in Denver, Patrick . . ." Brother Frank pauses. "Hey, you've been in Duffy's, Duffy's Irish Bar? They'd lock the doors at closing and we'd all go into a back room, get roaring drunk, sing Irish songs and jig 'til daylight. Hey, you can jig, Brother Patrick, can't you? I've heard you brag about it. Come on, let's see you jig."

Brother Patrick shakes his head, no.

"Come on, Patrick! I want to see you jig." Both are Irishmen, and Brother Patrick is often a target for Brother Frank's heckling. But Brother Patrick takes it good-naturedly, or else ignores him completely, and it gets Brother Frank's goat.

"Come on, I want to see you jig."

"I don't want to, Frank," Brother Patrick tells him.

Brother Vincent says, "Frank, how about a game of chess?"

"Brother Patrick's going to jig first, and then we'll see about your game of chess. He's dying to do it. He just wants us to coax him."

"Let him alone," Father Bede says.

"Father Bird, always looking out for his young," Brother Frank replies laughing. "Brother Patrick's been bragging to me for months now how he used to jig in his father's pub. Now he won't do it. Hell, I don't think he can. He's full of malarkey. You're all talk, Brother Malarkey. No guts at all. You're no Irishman, no countryman of mine."

I become more and more anxious for Brother Patrick. I know what would happen if Brother Frank kept heckling me. I'd get flustered and blow up, or just get up, walk out the door, and never show my face again.

"Why don't you stop pestering him, Frank," I tell him.

"It's no business of yours, Bill."

"It is my business, Frank. Patrick's a friend of mine. You are, too. You're always telling me to talk up, so I'm talking up."

The record ends. Brother Patrick gets up slowly, closes his missal, and sets his pipe down. He goes over and puts the needle back on. Facing us at the front of the room, he lifts the waist of his habit with both hands and holds it off the floor. And then, with his head high and his back very straight, he dances a lively jig.

If it isn't one thing, it's another

A loud rap on my door wakes me up the next morning in the middle of a dream about Martha. "Who is it?"

"It's me, Rosary Bede! Change your socks, smooth down your cowlick, let's slip out of here on the quick." He tells me he wants to drive in to Carlsbad to see some friends of his who are businessmen to ask if they will donate a rock-polishing machine. We want to polish the semi-precious stones we find in the valley and sell them in our shop.

But as we are getting into the car, Father Burkhart stops us. "Where do you think you're going, Father Bede?" he asks.

Father Bede tells him.

"Oh no, you're not, Father Bede. I want you to quit your running around. If you two are looking for something to do, get that old bus running and get it out of here."

He and Father Bede go into the friary, and I can't hear what they're saying, but when Father Bede comes out, he looks a little shaken. I feel humiliated for him.

"We can't go this morning, Bill," he says. "But don't be disappointed, buddy. We'll slip away sometime. Let's go clean up the porter's lodge, so we can set up our shop."

The porter's lodge is a two-room adobe building at the entrance to the monastery, originally intended for the gate keeper.

Stacked on shelves all around the room are reams of fresh paper of assorted colors and sizes that Brother Thomas has stored here for his print shop. It takes us several hours to gather it all up, stack it in cardboard boxes, and drag the boxes into the back room.

Then we wash all the windows. "It's a bright and sunny spot, isn't it, Father?"

Father Bede begins to sing in his beautiful tenor voice: "Brighten the corner where you are, lighten the corner where you are; someone far from harbor you may guide across the bar, brighten the corner where you are." Then he hands me the broom. "You sweep," he says, "the dust will dull the shine on my shoes."

Finally we're done. "Bill, let's put Tony's wooden covered wagon over there, it's our main attraction. The polished stones and petrified wood will look great on that table. Go get the grottoes, Bill. Let's see how they'll look."

When the grottoes Martha and her sisters made are lined up on the shelves, they stretch halfway around the room. "That's a lot of grottoes," I say. They remind me of the barn swallow nests we have back in Iowa.

"Yes, I got a little carried away on the grottoes, buddy. Here, have one."

"No thanks, I have one. Martha gave it to me. I guess I could have another one though."

"Of course you could, Bill. Or you may find a dozen of them between your sheets some night when you climb into bed.

"We'll have our official opening in the spring, Bill," he says. "And maybe we can hire Martha to clerk during the summer. You'd like *that*, wouldn't you? I've got some local pottery and weaving lined up. And one of the nuns at the convent with some training in art is going to teach the handicraft classes. It's all been arranged. I've looked forward to this for a long time."

"Lots of water colors and drawings from the school children, Father Bede. Maybe even a traveling exhibit."

"Tremendous idea!" he whoops. "We're in business, buddy."

"Open for business, plenty of bargains, grottoes, grottoes, grottoes! We'll have a 'Two-Fer,' Father."

"A what?"

" 'Two-Fer,' that's a two-for-the-price-of-one sale, like two tubes of toothpaste for the price of one. I learned that working in my uncle's drugstore, in a small, conservative, Amish-Mennonite farm town in Iowa. I didn't get a 'Two-Fer,' but I got a real bargain that winter.

"One morning, a beautiful girl came into the store, and my uncle introduced us. She was Mary, my second cousin. Later, my uncle told me confidentially that she was an outcast, 'jerk-over' Amish. That's a disparaging term the 'English' (that's what the Amish call us Yankees) use. In other words, she had broken the rules of the church and disgraced herself by wearing make-up and English clothes instead of the somber clothes the Amish wear."

"Loving God and feeling loved by Him is more important than church hierarchy," Father Bede says.

"I wanted to date Mary. My aunt laid down the law. Absolutely not. I could not date Mary, she was 'too worldly,' she would corrupt my morals. Furthermore, it would damage their reputation in the community and even hurt their drugstore. I was really annoyed.

"Instead, my aunt, against my protest, said she would arrange a date for me with a girl who sang in their church choir, Eudora

Bontrager, a 'golden Christian,' someone to 'share my strong faith and high ideals with.' I had neither. And I wasn't interested in Eudora.

"To entice me, she promised that if I would go out with Eudora just once, to 'share a good Christian experience,' and forget completely about Mary, she would give me an antique shoebox that I had coveted since I was a child.

"For that, I agreed.

"The night of our date arrived. Eudora was a stout farm girl with a plain face and big hands, who operated a lathe at the Yoder Tool and Die Company. We drove to a highway truckstop for coffee.

"We were both shy and neither one of us could think of anything to say. My uncle's suit was so loose on me that it attracted stares, the collar on his white shirt so tight I couldn't swallow, and his after shave still stung and made my nose run. Eudora was wearing jeans.

"We finished our coffee. Eudora had to get back; she worked the night shift. I dropped her off and went home to claim my reward. And there it was at the foot of my bed, the shoebox, walnut, upholstered on top, with a metal foot rest attached to the underside of the hinged lid, and with four solid brass griffins, half-eagle, half-lion, supporting the box on their wings. It was mine now, forever."

"That was both a funny and a sad experience, Bill. I enjoy your stories."

"I still feel sorry about Eudora; she never knew that she was swapped for an old shoebox."

Father Bede says, "You told me what a 'Two-Fer' sale is, Bill; I'll tell you what a 'Give-Away' sale is. Before you came here, I turned a corner of the porter's lodge into a rock shop—agates, pieces of opal, petrified wood, design specimens. I had to go away, so I put Patrick in charge; he had some idea, talking to me and others, what they were worth, so I told him, 'Get what you can but be reasonable!' "

"When I got back, he had sold everything. He was quite proud of himself. He's a delightful companion but he can goof things up. A black-carbon specimen that was worth a hundred dollars, he sold for five dollars. He got two dollars apiece for agates that were worth fifty or a hundred. He got a thousand dollars less than he should have."

Just then the door opens and Father Burkhart and Brother Thomas burst in. "Hey, my paper," Brother Thomas shouts. "I *knew* it, I *knew* it, I just *knew* it. Look, Father, they just dumped it in boxes, my entire stock of paper. It will take a month to re-sort it."

"We needed the space, Brother Thomas," Father Bede says. "I'm very sorry. I thought we were doing the right thing."

" 'Space!' " Brother Thomas says, "I'd like to see a thousand miles of it between you and this place."

"All right, that's enough, I don't want to hear anymore!" Father Burkhart scolds. "I want you all out of here for the time being. Stay out, shop or no shop, until I say so."

Numbed, I feel so sorry and humiliated again for Father Bede, and deeply disappointed. I want the shop, too. Father Bede is trying to do good, but sometimes he's a little impulsive. And Brother Thomas over reacted.

That evening Father Bede comes to my room. "Do your father and mother know you're mixed up with a bunch of crazy Catholics?"

I tell him yes, and he asks me what they think.

"They ask if I'm well, or if I'm getting enough to eat, that's about it."

"You must have fine parents," he says. "But it wasn't a very good day, was it, Bill?"

"No, very discouraging," I reply. "What are we going to do now?"

"Father Burkhart loves us. We'll just have to be patient, Bill."
"He's gruff and stern but I know he cares."
"Something will work out."
"I know it will, Father Bede. I'm sure it will."

He fishes in his pocket and drops a handful of change on my dresser top. "I thought maybe you could use some spending money. Perhaps you'd like to go in to Carlsbad some afternoon to look around."

"Thank you. No, I'd rather stay right here. There's no place else I'd rather be."

"It's good to hear you say that, Bill."

"I hear Father Bird finally got his wings clipped," Brother Frank says, when we are alone together in the friary that evening.

That makes me angry. "Roll up your pants' legs and make sure your own shorts are clean," I tell him.

*When you suddenly lose the best friend you've ever had,
you feel splintered and abandoned*

The following week Father Bede comes to my room after supper. There is a quiet knock on the door but no cheerful greeting.

"I'm afraid I have some bad news, Bill," he says. "I'm being transferred to Honduras in Central America."

"Are you really? I can't believe it."

"It's true, buddy."

"Why would you be transferred? What about all our projects? Do you really want to go?" All the good times we've had together flash through my mind, our hikes in the valley, our trips to Laro, the fun and the long talks. "What about our shop? And what about the Spanish? You're the only one around who cares about them and tries to help. Can't you just say you don't want to go?"

"I could, Bill, but when the Abbot gives an order, one obeys. Father Burkhart thinks I'm a run-around, always up to something new. It's hard, Bill. I'm not given much freedom. I want to reach out to other people and help them, you know how I am, and they want to leave the people alone."

"I know that," I say. "It doesn't seem fair to send you away. When do you have to leave?"

"I have to leave Monday, Bill."

"That's only two more days." I feel a sense of abject loss and abandonment.

"I've been ordered to leave, so I must."

"It's hard to imagine staying here if you're not here. I don't know what I'll do. Go somewhere and find a job. I think I can. I'm better than I was when I came here."

"I want to tell you something," he says, looking at me sternly. "There's more to you than what's on the surface, but who would ever know? You hide behind a wall of politeness, silence, and reserve, because you don't want others to know you. You're afraid you'll be hurt. You'll always be lonely. You'll have few friends. If you go on this way, drifting, you'll end up like one of those old derelicts who lived in your rooming house in Denver. You must risk to learn to walk, or to find out if you can walk a tightrope. I don't want to hear of your problems again, only of your health and daily attempts to conquer your fears. It's time to get off your butt and start living," he snaps.

I'm too stunned to speak.

He stands there a few minutes, then turns around without another word and walks out.

Memories of past failures and encounters come back. Father Bede's sharpness and rejection anger me.

I lie down on my bed. I've never felt such pain. I lie there until almost midnight. I get up, leave the room and go outside. The sky is brilliant and slowly my eyes adjust. I find my way to the friary, go inside, and feel my way to the double doors that lead to the courtyard. Light is coming from under the door of Father Bede's cell.

I rap on the door lightly.

"Bill!" he says softly, opening the door. "Come on in."

"Did I wake you?" I ask.

"Not really. I was reading and fell asleep in my chair."

"I want to talk to you. I don't like your telling me to get off my butt," I tell him abruptly, "or that I can't make friends, or that I don't have any friends."

Father Bede draws in his breath. "Bill," he says, "this is very good."

"What's good?" I ask.

"I gave you a challenge this evening and you failed to respond to it, and it angered me. But you *have* responded! You're here, and now we can talk. And you do have friends."

"What you said made me very angry," I reply. "I still am."

"Bill, I was trying to break through to an important area in your mind. Anger, hate, and fear are emotions that are part of all of us, and must not be buried. A lot of times our friendships are shallow, we say nice things, but we don't get below the surface. We need to be honest with our feelings or we can never truly love others on a level that is lasting and has meaning. Until you can share your feelings, good and bad, with others, you can never really know them, nor they you, and you will never see the richness and depth in another person's life. I was hard on you . . ."

"I swore at you. When you're close to someone it hurts so much to be angry at them that it makes you even angrier."

"You are loved, Bill. And God loves you; He loves you more than you love yourself. I was hard on you because I want the others to know you the way Frank, Patrick, and I do. They will love you, too. For weeks after you came here, I thought you were the most withdrawn kid I'd ever met. I could sense your loneliness in the tone of your voice and the things you told me about yourself. You've made progress, Bill. But you won't be here forever, and I want to know that when you leave you will be more aware of your own worth, so that you can begin to discover a sense of purpose and direction in your life, and make some good friends along the way."

Two days later, on a cold, gray afternoon I sit in the car waiting for Father Bede, to take him to Alejandro's to catch his bus. When he comes out he is wearing a cleaned and pressed black suit, his clerical collar, a black hat, and brightly polished shoes. It is a sad moment.

We are silent as we drive. Each familiar natural landmark we pass along the mountain road is a reminder that shortly I will be returning by the same route alone. I drive slowly, but for once Father Bede doesn't tell me I'm dragging the anchor.

"I remember," he says, "one night, quite late, I walked out to the gate to meet a young man on foot, who had trudged all the way from Laro. I will always remember that night."

"I will, too: 'Father Bede from Heaven.' I've learned a lot. And I've had the best time of my life. Knowing you will always be an influence on me. You've helped me so much."

"Bill, I'll want and need your help someday. Be patient, and pray we'll be together soon. Think about it, pray over it, and I'll contact you when I get set up. I'll have many tales to share with you when we see each other again, and I have many hopes for the future, which we'll map out; serving the sick and the poor, the hurt."

I carry his small black suitcase onto the bus. There are only two or three other passengers and I wish there were more. I watch the face of the bus driver as he checks the tickets, his expression impassive and indifferent.

"Remember, love others, and let others love you."

"Good-bye, Father Bede. I'll remember everything."

"God bless you, Bill. I love and trust you. Much depends upon God and your prayers. I have great confidence in you. You will probably have some problems along the way, but I think you'll find that you can make yourself do many things you thought you couldn't do before. You're better, but you still have so many fears. Put the fears out and bring in joy and happiness. You'll have friends anywhere you go!"

I drive back to the monastery feeling utterly alone. Do Father Burkhart and the Abbot realize how much good Father Bede was really doing for others, especially the Spanish? How could they tear him away from his work, his home, and his friends, and ship him off to another continent?

And yet, wasn't the purpose of monastic life to allow a man to become separate from, and to keep him from having contact with, the material world? He needed to concentrate all of his energies towards a closer union with God. And wasn't Father Bede obliged, then, through his vow of obedience, to take orders from his superior, Father Burkhart?

But I marvel at Father Bede's acceptance: He leaves without anger or bitterness, believing in himself and in what he thinks is right, completely open to the challenge of a new adventure.

". . . Thou hast destroyed cities; their memorial is perished with them" — Psalm IX

The afternoon of the following day, Brother Frank comes to my room and asks me to go with him to visit the pueblo ruins.

"I've got to get out of here for a while," he says, startling me by the tone of his voice and the look on his face. I hesitate because I'm afraid we'll get in trouble with Father Burkhart, but I'm disturbed by the tone of desperation in his voice, so I tell him I'll go.

He tells me to go get Father Alfonse's flashlight so we can explore the dark, underground kivas.

"Oh, no, can't we get along without it?" I ask, remembering Father Alfonse's obsessive attachment to his flashlight.

"Get going, Bill, we don't have all day."

I run down to the laundry room. "Oh dear, what for?" Father Alfonse asks, his voice shaky. "Well, I guess so. Could you bring it back before dark, please? The batteries could run low. It might break if you drop it."

It is indeed a fancy flashlight with a color-filter that can be twisted to yellow, green or red. "The red is for signalling in an emergency," Father Alfonse explains.

"What took you so long?" Brother Frank barks when I get back.

"Father Alfonse had to show me how to use it. I didn't want to be rude."

When we get to the pueblo, Brother Frank says it's the off-season for tourists and we'll have to ask for permission. "If they won't let us in, we'll sneak in," he says. "You be quiet and let me do the talking."

Brother Frank smooth talks the caretakers, a little, elderly Anglo couple who live there the year around. He rattles on like a college professor about the history and anthropology of the area. The old lady is impressed and asks, "Do you study about that in the monastery?" Then she brings us cookies and tea. I am afraid we won't get away before the sun goes down.

"Where did you learn all that?" I ask Brother Frank afterwards.

"I read," he snaps. "And once I was a researcher for *Compton's Encyclopedia*."

It is a cold, bleak, winter day, no snow, quite in harmony with the eerie feeling one gets looking out across the windy, desolate, rock-strewn mesa, where the pueblo village once stood, to the stark ruins of a mission church, and large conical mounds of earth marking the underground ceremonial houses, or kivas, which are entered by a ladder through a hole in the roof.

I pick up some shards on the ground which are decorated with heavy black dots and lines.

"Don't take those," Brother Frank says sharply. "They don't belong to you."

A moment later I see him pick one up, examine it, and slip it into his pocket. "It's okay," he says, "no one can see us."

As we walk along, Brother Frank explains that "pueblo" is the Spanish word for village. He tells me that the pueblo, probably built in the 1300s, had once been a five-story dwelling. "It had a wooden balcony around it and you could walk around the entire village without setting foot on the ground."

We crawl through the hatchway in the conical roof of a kiva and climb down the wooden ladder by the light of Father Alfonse's flashlight. In one wall is a shaft for fresh air. In the center of the kiva is a pit. Brother Frank says it served as the entrance to a place in the depths of the earth from which the sacred gods emerged.

He tells me how the Spanish conquistadors had come from Mexico in search of gold; attacked the pueblos and even destroyed them; forced the Indians to give up their religion and Christianized them.

"Father Bede says you conquer people with love, not swords," I say. "Why didn't the Spanish leave these people alone?"

"You've got a lot to learn about the world, Bill," Brother Frank replies. "The modern-day Pueblo Indians still hate the Spanish. You and I could visit a pueblo, but they'd never let a Spaniard set foot inside. The Spanish who live here today are the descendants of those Spanish conquistadors. They've owned this land for hundreds of years."

"So the land once belonged to the Pueblos, before it belonged to the Spanish, and now a lot of it belongs to the Anglos, and the Spanish resent *them* for encroaching," I say.

"That's about it," Brother Frank replies. "It's dog eat dog, tooth and asshole, in this world. If I'd had you in my platoon during the war, I'd have shown you what the world is really like."

"I'm glad I wasn't. I don't need to stick my nose in a lot of spilled guts to know what the world's like."

We walk through the ruins of the large mission church with four-foot thick, red adobe walls and a maze-like series of rooms.

Brother Frank points to a section of the chancel wall, just behind the altar.

"If you dug in that spot," he says, "you'd probably find the chalice and the vestments. That's where they were likely buried. You and I will come back here with a pickaxe some night and do a little excavating."

I ask Brother Frank to stand in front of the church so I can take his picture, but he won't let me. "I'm wanted by the F.B.I.," he says.

When we get back to the monastery, I ask Brother Patrick about that. "The other day," Brother Patrick says, "Frank brought me this old copy of *Life* and showed me a story about the Mafia. Frank said, 'Read this. T'ats what I was, after the war, a hatchet man.' "

Sadly but inevitably, the road divides

On the way back from the pueblo ruins I am surprised to find out that Brother Frank takes Father Bede's leaving as hard as I do.

Frank, who still seems troubled, has been lost in thought.

"Well, so much for Father Bede," he says finally.

"How do you mean?" I ask. "I hated to see Father Bede go. But he wasn't transferred, he was ousted, wasn't he?"

"Yes, you could say that," he snaps. "Sometimes I think you know more about the world than you let on. I'm going to make life a little difficult for Father Burkhart when the time comes."

"I know you were very close to Father Bede, Frank, and I know how much he thought of you."

I am reminded of something Father Bede said to me once. "Frank has his problems. I give him books to read that I think will help him, but he reads so far, gets discouraged because he thinks he can't reconcile what he reads with what he believes, and is too impatient to read far enough to get the real meaning. I love that guy, but he demands so much of my time that it almost does me in."

"I'm leaving," I say. "Monday or Tuesday."

"You're what?" Frank exclaims.

"I've got to go out and try to make it on my own. Besides, it won't be the same around here without Father Bede. I'll miss you, too, Frank," I tell him.

"What's your hurry?" he asks. "You've got a roof over your head and three meals."

"Even so," I reply. "I'm leaving."

"I think you ought to stick around a while longer. Deer season opens in eight days. I'm going to shoot myself a nice fat buck. We'll have some venison steak."

"I'm not much interested in deer hunting," I say.

Frank turns to me. "I'm leaving, too. We'll leave here together, you and I. After deer season. We need each other's company. We can help each other. We'll stick together."

"What do you mean? Go some place together?"

"My old man owns a garage. It's a small town and the pace is slow. I'm a trained mechanic. You could pump gas and patch a tire, couldn't you? He's got some old tourist cabins. They're not too fancy, but you could have one, rent free, fix it up the way you like."

I am flattered and dumbfounded. Brother Frank has been a friend and helped me, but I had no idea he thought of me as an equal or that he valued my friendship.

"Thank you, Frank," I tell him. "That makes me feel good. I'll stay on until deer season, and think about what you said."

Brother Frank becomes more restless and irritable in the following days. He doesn't talk to anyone, just keeps to himself and doesn't even come to recreation.

Almost everything annoys him. "Bill, stay away from Brother Patrick," he warns me: "This morning he said, 'Hey, Frank, hold this board for me so I can saw it.' I did and he almost cut my hand off. That guy is completely reckless. I think he did it deliberately." Or, "Brother Thomas left a package of frozen meat on the floor of the walk-in freezer. I tripped on it and almost broke my neck. I think he did it on purpose. I've got a good mind to take him out behind the barn and teach him a lesson."

Brother Frank's concern for his cats is adding to his problems. I stumble over a dead cat as I am carrying an armload of wood for the stove in Brother Thomas's print shop. I tell Brother Thomas about it.

"Those damn cats, they're everywhere," he says. "The place is overrun with Frank's cats. Father Burkhart is sick of them. He doesn't want 'em in the courtyard, either. Frank rounds 'em up at night and herds 'em into the courtyard so Big Boy can't get at 'em. But someone always forgets and leaves the door open," he says, grinning. "Big Boy gets in. I found another dead cat this morning besides the one you found. That makes six. I'll bet we'll find the yard littered with dead cats when the snow melts."

Well, Brother Thomas, I think to myself, you've got your record player and country-western records, Father Alfonse has his flashlight, Brother Patrick had his bicycle, Father Bede his bus, and what's wrong if Brother Frank has a few cats?

"I feel sorry for Brother Frank," I say. "He acts troubled; I'm worried. I wish there was some way to help him. I know he misses Father Bede."

"We don't miss Father Bede, and we won't miss Frank, either, when he's gone."

"I'll chop up some more wood, Brother Thomas," I tell him, and leave.

On top of everything else, Brother Frank has caught the flu. He tips loaves all day in front of a hot oven and then walks back and forth to meals in his T-shirt in the middle of the winter. He picks at his food or skips meals. I offer to bring his meals to his cell but he tells me to stay away, I might catch what he has.

"Brother Patrick, I need some of that altar wine," I hear him tell Brother Patrick. "I haven't touched a drop since I came here except at Thanksgiving, but I need some now. What's wrong with a little wine if it'll help my stomach?"

Brother Patrick sighs and says, "Oh, Frank, I wouldn't do that," relights his pipe and goes on his way.

Later, upstairs in the friary, I overhear Father Burkhart tell Brother Vincent, "I want you to lock the vestry door tonight and bring me the key. Frank is not going to touch a drop of wine. Has he forgotten the pledge he made?"

The next morning before breakfast Brother Frank comes to my room to ask if I have any magazines. I tell him I'm sorry but I don't.

"I don't have any money, Bill, but would you do me a favor? Would you go to Alejandro's and buy me a newspaper and a *Life* or *Time*? But leave them here in your room. Don't bring them to me, I'll read them here."

I am startled that he would ask me to buy him magazines, but most of all I am upset by his abject manner. I can see he is deeply troubled. His longing for news of the outside world is, I think, an indication of his anguish and indecision.

"Of course I will, Frank, if you want me to." I am fond of Brother Frank, and will always remember his kindnesses to me. I envy him. I'd like to be as savvy and tough as he is, but with his feeling and compassion, too. I hope we are still going to Georgia together, to work in his father's garage, but I know what a difficult decision this is for Frank.

"Thanks, Bill. You'll always be my friend. You give a damn about other people, most people only give a damn about themselves. You're better than you think you are. And you can be trusted. I've always known that."

I go and buy the magazines and a candy bar for Frank and bring them back to my room where he is waiting, then I excuse myself and go take a long walk to leave him alone.

Sometimes in your self-doubt you don't really know how much someone cares for you until she comes to say good-bye

After Vespers this evening, on the way to my room, I'm startled when I hear, or think I hear, my name called softly from somewhere in the shadows as I am inching my way along in the dark without a flashlight.

Petrified, I freeze, then I hear it again, "Bill," from a few feet away. A flashlight clicks on.

"Who is it?"

"Me . . . it's me, Martha."

"Martha? You scared the daylights out of me," I exclaim. "I can't see you, where are you? Have you been here very long?"

"For a while. I wass waiting for you, I haf to tell you some-theeng," she says tearfully.

"Martha, what's wrong?"

"I feel very bad, Bill. I can't see you anymore. I jus' want to tell you 'good-bye,' then I haf to go."

"Tell me what's wrong, Martha. Come on in. There's a light in the hall. It's a little warmer, too."

We step inside the door and I find the light switch.

"Don't look at me, Bill," she says, shielding her eyes, red and swollen, with her hand.

"I'm sorry. I won't. But you look very pretty, just like you always do. What happened, Martha, can you tell me?"

"When I brought you the tortillas the other day, Felix came weeth me like my mother say he ees supposed to do . . . but then I told heem . . . he didn't do wat I told heem . . ."

Felix had tagged along, that was the rule, but only part of the way because Martha had persuaded him, for twenty cents, to sit down on a rock somewhere between her house and the monastery and wait there for her. Martha wasn't gone long, just long enough to bring me the tortillas and talk for a few minutes, but when she got back to the spot where she had left Felix, he wasn't there. He had gotten restless and gone back home.

"Mother ees angry with me and she say that I can't see you anymore." Martha starts crying again.

"Never?" I ask, stunned.

"She say I lied to her. I did."

I remember what Father Bede told me about the Corrillo family, how they upheld the old Spanish values and traditions, including strict respect for and obedience to parents, and knowing this I understand why Martha is distraught.

"Does your mother know you're here?"

"No, mother ees with my sister who lives in Carlsbad. She jus' had a baby and mother went to help her with the other children," Martha says, giving me a long lingering look the way she always does. No girl has ever done that to me before. I try to hold my eyes on hers. Her face is soft and hauntingly beautiful.

I can't let her go without telling her how I feel about her, but I can't find the right words. I'm getting ready to give her a good-bye hug. But just as I reach for her, she jumps into my arms and clings to me tightly: "What's that noise, Bill!"

"That scraping sound?" I ask, trying to catch my breath. "That's just the cows, Martha. They come up here at night to eat the grass in the yard, and they brush against the building to scratch their hides."

Martha is still in my arms. My face burns where it touches her face. Pressed against her, I can feel her breasts through the material of her clothing, her heartbeat, the warmth of her body, her thighs against mine. My heart beats like a hummingbird's wings. I haven't allowed myself to have any sexual fantasies about Martha because of her kindness and her interest in me, afraid that having sexual desires towards her would be a betrayal of our trust and respect for each other, but I am having them now.

I stroke her hair tentatively but I can tell she likes it, then I kiss her and she kisses me back.

"I teenk I am falling in love with you, Bill," she whispers.

"I love you, Martha." I have never said that to a girl before, but it comes easily.

"You are deefferent than the boys I know. I like the way you talk to me and tell me things, and listen to me. The other boys don't do that. You are very shy but I like that, too."

"Let's go to Denver, Martha. Or anyplace you want. I'll find a job and I'll take care of you."

"My father haf promised me he will send me to art school in Albuquerque next year when I graduate here. Comb to see me there, Bill, and we can be together. I want to be with you and make you happy the way you make me happy."

"That seems like such a long time away, but I will, I promise. I want to be with you, too."

"Now I haf to go, Bill."

I feel an aching, panicky sense of loss. We hug each other, whisper good-bye, and she slips out the door.

Following the beam of Martha's flashlight trailing off into the night, I have a sudden remembrance, summer vacation trips in the family car, the endless highway, how in my imagination I'd reach out with my arm and try to clip off each telephone pole as it sped by, as if I might reach out the same way now and grab the beam and pull it and Martha back to me.

Will I ever see her again? I must. All that matters to me is Martha. But a year is a long time, and life, I already know, is as unpredictable as Felix's dilapidated motorscooter.

"Giving this bunch rifles and putting them on horseback is about as safe as backing off an exit ramp on an icy freeway" — Brother Frank

Heavy snow fills the passes. Father Burkhart and Brothers Vincent, Thomas, and Frank, who is now over the flu, prepare for a week of deer hunting in the mountains.

A day or two before the season opens, I go to the print shop with my daily armload of wood, and there sits Brother Thomas admiring a lever-action Winchester that looks brand new. I know that the vow of poverty doesn't allow personal possessions, and I ask him where he got it.

"It belongs to my dad," he says, grinning. "I'm just taking care of it for him until after deer season."

"I didn't know monks hunted," I say.

"Yup, Father Burkhart likes to hunt and so do the rest of us. Besides, if we're lucky, we'll have enough venison to last us most of the winter. A friend of Father Burkhart's has a two-thousand acre ranch in the mountains. We hunt on horseback. He invites us every year."

"Ahf t'ey go, like a pack o' starved 'ounds," Brother Patrick says to me after breakfast the next morning.

"Oh my," Father Alfonse sighs. "They forget to empty their pockets and those bullets end up in my washing machine."

The first day of hunting Brother Frank shoots a huge buck. Brother Thomas and Brother Vincent each get one the second day.

But the days pass and the season grows shorter, and Father Burkhart comes home empty-handed each evening.

"I'm worried 'bout 'im," I hear Brother Patrick tell Brother Frank. "'E's a proud man, 'e is, 'n' it's 'ard on 'im when these younger men show 'im up. The strain and exertion aren't too good for 'im."

There is no levity at the dinner table and Brother Thomas and Brother Vincent are subdued. They look up from their plates and their eyes meet and they glance solicitously at Father Burkhart, who leans wearily over the table on his elbows, unshaven, his food untouched, staring at the wall with a glazed look and sighing like the airbrakes on a diesel truck.

Everyone suffers when Father Burkhart is unhappy. He lumbers around with his shoulders hunched and his head bowed, barking orders. And when he goes into his cell, he slams the door so hard you can hear it across the valley.

On the last day of the hunting season, however, Father Burkhart shoots a deer.

"Hmmph," he grunts absentmindedly at the table this evening, grinning and shaking his head, as he re-lives the day's events.

"Damn!" he says, snapping his fingers, and finally dispensing with the ban on talking. "I knew I'd get my deer. Pow, one shot. An hour before the season closed."

"Father was going nuts to get a deer," Brother Frank whispers to me. "He couldn't stand it that the rest of us got ours."

"I get my deer every season," Father Burkhart continues.

"Yeah, I saw your deer," Brother Frank says. "One of the cats was dragging it around. I think she left it behind the refrigerator."

Father Burkhart's face flushes. "I'll have you know I shot that deer at two hundred yards," he snaps angrily, pointing his finger at Brother Frank.

"Sure. But it was just a spike. That's the size you make pets out of. Nobody shoots spikes."

The rest of us suddenly busy ourselves with little things, brushing away crumbs, stacking our dishes. Brother Frank just sits there laughing.

Later on that evening Brother Frank comes to my room. "Bill, have you been in the barn?" he asks sharply.

Right away I guess what has happened. "Oh no, not Minny?"

"That's right," he says, "someone left the door open, *wide* open. Big Boy got her."

I know how much Minny meant to Brother Frank. A few weeks before I came to the monastery, Big Boy had gotten into the courtyard and broken her back. Father Burkhart had ordered Brother Frank to kill her, but he hadn't. Instead, he had carried her to the barn and taped her up in a body splint. He had hand fed her. When she was healed, he taught her how to walk again by putting a hand under her belly to support her. He had invited me to come to the barn with him to see her once. I was shocked. Her back was horribly twisted and bowed, her head jutting out from her body at an odd angle and her neck rigid. Wild-eyed and gaunt, she walked with a sideways, stiff-legged gait, the fur on her back missing in clumps. The noise she made was a shrill screech, no longer cat-like.

I'll bet Frank's been through a mauling or two himself, I had thought to myself.

"Don't ever come in here and leave the door open," he had warned me. "And don't tell anyone she's in here."

Now, what Brother Frank had feared, has happened.

"I haven't been in the barn since you showed her to me, Brother Frank," I tell him. "I feel sick about it."

"I know it wasn't you, Bill. But I know who it *was*. Father

Burkhart or his brother, Thomas."

"I don't think so, Frank."

"I *know* so. Father Burkhart and I are going to have a little talk. I've dealt with men like him before."

For days Brother Frank broods silently about Minny. He doesn't join in the talk at lunch where talking is permitted, and he doesn't come to recreation. Instead, he is out in the dark with Father Alfonse's flashlight, tinkering with Father Bede's bus.

"What would you do if you were me?" I hear him ask Brother Patrick. "I *know* it's Brother Thomas who left the door open. He did it deliberately. I loved that cat and he killed it. I think I'll take him out in back of the barn and teach him a lesson."

Brother Patrick just listens and puffs on his pipe and won't say a thing.

Breadcrumbs for beer is a good trade

The next day, Saturday, Brother Frank comes to my room after lunch. "Bill, get your car going, we're going to take Joe some breadcrumbs from the bakery for his chickens and trade them for candy." Frank has a sweet tooth for licorice. Joe is a Spanish farmer who lives in the mountains and owns a small grocery store. I back my car up to the bakery and we load cardboard boxes full of breadcrumbs into the trunk. Then we start up the mountain.

The road climbs steeply. A soft snow is falling and in the distance the scrub pine look like dark stubble against the white ground. Directly below us, beyond a sheer drop of four-hundred feet, lies the valley, wild, bleak, and gray. Ahead are distant snow-capped peaks.

Brother Frank looks very rugged, handsome too, in his blue jeans and denim jacket. I like to be around him, am flattered that he likes my company, and I am happy we are going somewhere together, but his silence makes me uneasy.

"It's time for me to deal with Brother Thomas and Father Burkhart," he says abruptly, startling me.

"Are you still angry at them?" I ask.

"That's right, *you* don't get angry, do you," he says sarcastically.

"You know that's not true, Frank. I won't even answer that."

I'm half afraid of Brother Frank when he's upset.

"Don't ever let anyone push you around," he says. "You'll never have any self-respect if you do. Do you think anyone really gives a damn what you say or do? You suffer more from keeping things locked in your guts than you would from any harm that might come to you from saying what you think. Perhaps you ought to stay here at the monastery for the rest of your life so the world can't harm you, so you can be protected."

"I told you I was leaving, Frank. You wanted me to stick around till after deer season. We're friends, aren't we? I don't want or need protection. You're always trying to tell me, and Brother Thomas, too, what the world is really like—you know, 'dog eat dog, tooth and asshole.' Then what's wrong with being attracted to this place, to want to reject the world, the meanness and cruelty?

"I've made friends here, on my own, that's the best part. People I admire, especially you, Father Bede, and Patrick, the first real friends I've had. I wouldn't trade that for anything. I can talk to you, Frank. I tell you things I've never told anyone before."

"That's good," he says, calming down.

"I've learned some things, too, and don't feel as much at odds with myself as I did before. The world's bigger and broader than I thought it was; bigger than that damn hotel in Denver; bigger, too, than that midwest town I come from.

"I like it here. I've never felt happier, and I'll still feel that way when I'm out of here."

When we get to Joe's, Brother Frank and I unload the bread-crumbs on the cement stoop in front of the store.

"Wait here, I'll be right out," he says.

"I'll come along."

"No, you wait here."

I get back into the car. There is a rotting deer head nailed to a Dr. Pepper sign fastened to a tree next to the road, and at the bottom of the sign, pock-marked with rifle slugs, it says 'Joe's' in sloppy, hand-painted letters. The store is in the front of Joe's shack. It is in an isolated, wooded area at the edge of the narrow mountain road.

Ten minutes later Brother Frank comes back out with a bulging paper sack, cradling it carefully.

"Did you make a good trade?" I ask.

"A damn good one," Brother Frank says laughing.

The road is slippery from the falling snow as we drive back down the mountain, and I drive cautiously. It would be a good afternoon, I think to myself, to be sitting on the wooden bench in front of a fire back in the friary, watching the snow fall in the courtyard.

Brother Frank opens the sack—there is no candy in it—takes out a miniature bottle of brandy, drinks it in one swallow, jerks the window down and chucks the bottle out. "I've been trying to get you mad, but I can't do it," he says.

"Why should I be mad?" I ask.

"Do you ever pray?"

"Yes, I pray. I never prayed until I came here to the monastery. Sometimes it's a great comfort, sometimes it doesn't comfort me. I keep trying, almost with every breath."

He opens a second bottle, tosses it down, cranks the window down and whips the empty out with great force. "When I pray," he says, "I just kneel on the floor and pray. I don't expect to float around the room or to be lifted off my knees. Maybe you expect too much."

"I'm not expecting miracles. What I'm inspired by is Father Bede's faith and his love of others and wanting to help them. He helped me, that I know."

"Hurray for Father Bird. You don't have *him* to lead you around anymore. I'll tell you something. You don't have any spine."

"What do you mean by that?" I ask, trying not to let Frank provoke me.

"You don't get mad, you bottle everything inside. You don't know *how* to hate. You've got to learn how to hate. You've got to hate and hate, before you can love God. And when you love God, you've got to jump in head and shoulders."

"I get mad and I know how to hate, I've told you that," I reply. "Why don't you get off my back?"

"Good, you *are* mad. Your face is red."

"Can I have one of those bottles?" I ask. "Just one."

"I didn't think you drank, Bill, or you could've had one earlier." Then he asks me if I have any money and I tell him I have a few dollars. "When we get to town, we'll stop by Alejandro's, and you'll go in and buy us a six-pack of beer and a fifth of good brandy. I don't want anyone to see me go in there."

"I don't have much money on me," I say, trying to dissuade him. "You know you shouldn't drink, Frank."

"I'll decide that!" he says angrily.

When we get to Alejandro's, I go in and buy the beer and brandy. Brother Frank tells me where to drive. We end up a quarter of a mile up a firetrail in the mountains near the monastery, so we can sit in the car and he can drink without being observed.

"I feel more confident when I drink. Do you?" he asks in a gentle tone of voice.

"Yes, I do." His candor touches me. He isn't angry anymore and I feel close to him again.

"I'm getting out of here tonight, Bill," he says finally. "But first I'm going to get even with Brother Thomas and Father Burkhart."

"Don't slug anyone, Frank. You can't solve anything that way. Talk it out with them."

"It's my business how I handle those two," he says angrily.

"Where will you go, Frank? Home to Georgia? Work in your dad's garage?"

"Mexico." He takes a deep swallow of brandy. "I want you to come with me, Bill. We'll travel, live in the cantinas, and I'll show you what life is really like. I've got friends we can stay with. We'll drive your car to El Paso, leave it in a garage, and hitch rides the rest of the way."

I know Brother Frank could show me adventure and life on the road that I would never see on my own. I would meet people and encounter situations that I'd never experience in my tame world, and go places my timid legs would never take me. And with the thought of losing Brother Frank as a friend, I can already feel a deep loneliness.

"No, I can't, Frank, as much as I'd like to. It's very tempting, but I have other plans."

Father Bede is gone. Brother Frank is the best friend I have, and now I'll lose him.

"I heard you tell Father Bede once you'd like to go to Mexico," he continues. "Some kid wanting you to fuck his sister or sell you Spanish fly, that's all you'd find. I'll show you what the country is really like. I'll show you how to take care of yourself, too. Do you have the guts?"

"It would be a choice for me, not just guts," I reply. "But I wouldn't want to leave the way you want to; I mean I wouldn't want to explode and hurt someone, like Brother Thomas or Father Burkhart. Father Bede didn't leave that way."

"I'll handle it my way, but you stay out of it. Are you coming with me or not?"

"I wish I could, but I don't think I can."

"Were you living at home when you were going to that college in Iowa where your father was Dean?"

"Yes."

"And all these quit-and-run jobs of your's, were you living at home then, too?"

"Yes. Until I came to Denver."

"You've been completely on your own for how long now?"

"About eight months."

"What are your plans when you leave here, when you leave the protection of the monastery? Float around, quit this job, quit that one? Or will you crawl back home with your tail between your legs? I think you should come with me."

"No, I'm not going back home." Before I came to the monastery, I ached for the security of home, and at moments I still do, and I will even more, I know, when I leave the monastery, but I'm not going back home.

"What will you do?"

"Father Bede says he has great faith in me. He's given me confidence. He says I'm no failure. He says he wants and needs my help. If and when that day comes, I'll be ready. In the meantime, I'm thinking through some plans that include a job."

"Are you? Or will you fold again the first time someone calls you fart or swish, raises his voice, or looks at you cross-eyed?"

That stings. But I like Brother Frank so much that he can't make me angry anymore, and besides, it's a fair question.

"I think you are desperate to find yourself. You're a nervous, frightened kid. I told you I could show you how to take care of yourself. It could make a man out of you. If you don't, you'll likely be a timid, fearful cripple the rest of your life."

"I told you about Dr. Mason's Feelings Group, Frank. That's what I'm going to do. I'm going to Carlsbad, find myself a job, and get into the Feelings Group. I know I need help, and I'm going to get it. It won't be easy, but I know I have to force myself to do it."

"You'll be in with a bunch of hinder-hoppers and menopausal females and you'll all sit around in a tight little circle and re-enforce each other's hang-ups."

"I don't think that's fair, Brother Frank. I trust Dr. Mason. There will be people of all ages and occupations. And I have the opportunity now of facing my problems head-on, once and for all, I hope."

"If you go with me," Brother Frank says, "you'll learn about life and you won't need that Feelings Group." He passes the bottle. "Take a sip, Bill. Then let's get going, it's late. Your hair looks like hell and I want to cut it before Vespers. Hide the brandy in your dresser drawer and don't tell anyone what we've talked about. I'll come by your room later tonight. You can let me know then if you're going with me. But stay in your room after supper until I get there!"

When we get back, Brother Frank clips my hair, while I sit in the barber chair in the basement in front of the window that looks out on the stark, snowy fields and, beyond, the gray wooded banks of the river. It is dim and silent in the basement. I sit there feeling anxious and depressed, remembering Father Bede, worrying about Brother Frank. The temptation to leave with Frank is great, but I fight it.

When Frank is done, he brushes the hair off my neck, goes to Vespers, and I go back to my room to clean up for supper.

"Put away the evil one among you" —
*1 Corinthians 5:13, and "if the faithless one depart, let
him depart"* — *1 Corinthians 7:15*

The chair next to me at the supper table this evening is empty. It's Frank's chair. Father Burkhart gives me a long, hard look that makes me feel very uncomfortable. After supper Brother Patrick stops me in the friary. "Brother Frank acts strange," he says in a low voice. "'E came ta Vespers late, 'n' started singin' the wrong verses. Then 'e started laughin'. Where is 'e? Why didn't 'e come ta supper? I'm worried, I am."

Alarmed, I tell him I don't know and hurry back to my room. With a shock, the first thing I notice is Brother Frank's black habit folded over the back of my chair. I open the dresser drawer, and the bottle of brandy, two-thirds full when I put it there, is empty. Next to it is the $5.00 that Brother Frank said he would pay me back. I stand there for a few minutes, stunned. Where is Frank now? What's happened to him?

I hear footsteps in the hall, there's a rap on the door, and in rush Brothers Vincent and Patrick. Brother Patrick's face is ashen.

"Where did you and Frank go this afternoon?" Brother Vincent asks anxiously.

I tell him we drove up to Joe's.

"Did Frank have anything to drink?"

"Oh, God, what's wrong?" I ask.

Brother Vincent says, "I just got back from Laro, and it's lucky I did. If I'd gotten back a minute later, it might have been too late. I walked into Brother Thomas's cell and there was Brother Thomas on his knees, and Frank had Father Burkhart's .30-06 pointed at his head. The clip was jammed and he was fumbling with it. I shouted at him and he looked up, said 'son-of-a-bitch,' tossed the gun at me, and ran out. I couldn't catch him."

"Is Brother Thomas all right?" I ask.

"He was when I left him."

"Where is Brother Thomas now?"

"I don't know. He's hiding somewhere."

"What about Father Burkhart?"

"Frank gave Father Burkhart quite a scare," Brother Patrick says. "'E roughed 'im up a bit, 'e did, 'n' took 'is deer rifle."

"Where is Brother Frank?"

"We don't know," Brother Vincent says. "We've got to find him before he gets into *real* trouble. Lock your door and stay here in your room."

"Frank wouldn't hurt me," I say.

Just then we hear a shrill blast.

"What the 'ell is t'at?" Brother Patrick asks. Then we hear it again, twice more.

Brother Vincent runs out the door and in a few minutes he is back. "It's Frank. He's got Father Bede's bus running and he's up in the yard. He's too drunk to drive; he knocked down the statue of Our Lady. He's up to something. He went around the corner of the friary towards the pasture. Good Lord, Brother Thomas's print shop!" He and Brother Patrick run out the door.

I sit down on the edge of the bed, dazed, trying to figure things out. I can't believe that Frank would really try to kill Brother Thomas.

It is quiet and still again, like any other evening at the monastery, as if what has happened is a dream, and any minute the chapel bell will ring to call us to Complin.

I sit there anxiously, wondering what has happened, where Brother Thomas is and if he's all right, and where Brother Patrick and Brother Vincent have gone.

Then I hear the front door open, running footsteps in the hall, and Brother Thomas bursts into my room, out of breath.

"Frank's . . . after . . . me. He's out there somewhere. He's gone off the deep end. He's crazy. He tried to shoot me. Then he smashed all the windows in the friary. He wants to fight but I don't want to. I don't want to mess with him. If he comes near me, Bill, and I have to, I'll shoot him. I've got a gun inside my habit," he says, unsnapping the waist to show me a derringer. "Does your door lock?"

"No, it doesn't."

"I'll hide in your closet."

I ask where Father Burkhart and the others are and he says, "They're down in the recreation room and they've got the door locked. I knocked but I can't get in."

Brother Thomas jumps into the closet and shuts the door. I sit there wondering what's going to happen, worried that Brother Thomas might shoot Brother Frank if he comes to my room. A few minutes later my door flies open and Brother Frank stumbles in. I can't tell how drunk he is, but he has such a driving energy about him that I stand well out of the way.

"Where's Brother Thomas?" he shouts. "I want that bastard."

"I don't know where he is," I answer him, frightened. "He's not around here!"

"You're lying. I saw him come in here." Brother Frank scoops up my chair by the leg with one hand and brings it down on top of the dresser, smashing it into kindling.

"He did come in here," I say. "But he ran out the back door."

"I'll find him."

"Cut it out, leave him alone," I shout.

"Keep out of my way, Bill, I'd hate to hurt you."

Desperately trying to think of some way to stop him, I say, "I thought we were going to Mexico. If we are, let's get going."

"We are," he says, quieting down a little, "but first I want Brother Thomas."

"You'll never find him, Frank. You scared him. He's long gone by now."

Brother Frank laughs. "I'll find him. That bastard will surface *sometime* tonight."

"He's probably down in the pasture hiding, Frank. You couldn't even find him in the daylight. Let's get out of here!"

Brother Frank totters and falls onto the edge of the bed. "Piss on it, he's not worth the trouble," he says, his speech slurred. "I fixed him anyway. I ass-ended that bus of Father Bede's right into his print shop. I'll come back and get him when I'm sober. Tell him that. It'll give him something to think about. Let me rest a minute," he says, breathing hard. "Then I'll go get some religious clothes; it's easier to hitch rides that way."

He leaves. I throw my clothes into the back seat of my car; I know I'm not going to Mexico with Brother Frank, but I know I have to get him out of here, and I don't know where we might end up. I take along the rosary Father Bede blessed and gave me.

In a few minutes Brother Frank comes back, no longer in jeans and a T-shirt, but in a black suit with a clerical collar, black hat, and carrying a duffel bag, the same way Father Bede was dressed when he left.

I'm startled by the priest's collar and ask him where he got it as we're getting into the car, but he doesn't answer.

The night is black and cold. We drive down the mountain into Laro, past the convent, the statue of Our Lady of Guadalupe looking like an apparition in its cold floodlight, through town, past Alejandro's, and head across the dark desert towards the highway six miles beyond, not so far from the spot where my Chevy broke down on a bright fall morning months ago.

"Let me give you a ride to Carlsbad, Brother Frank. Get yourself a room there tonight, so you can start out fresh in the morning," I say.

"No, we're going tonight."

"I'm not going. I don't want to travel this way. Besides, I told you my plans."

"What do you mean, 'this way'?"

"You're drunk. And I'm afraid of you when you do what you did tonight."

"Hell, they'll never let you come back either. But if you've made up your mind and you're not coming with me, drive me to the highway."

"Do you have any money?" I ask, after a while.

Brother Frank laughs. "How in the hell would I have any money? Don't worry too much about that."

"Brother Frank, send me your address when you get to Mexico. Then we can keep in touch."

"Don't call me 'Brother,' " he says angrily. "I'm no Brother anymore. No, I won't do that. It's now or never." He pauses. "You're a spineless pawn and I used you today."

"I'm not a pawn, Frank. You didn't use me. That's an excuse. I bought the liquor, but you drank it."

"I've killed more than one man in my time, and I could kill you too, you punk," Frank says.

I feel a sense of unreality and my mind whirls. Then something comes to me.

"I'd better stop and check the oil," I say, braking. "I don't want to run the car out of oil again. I've got cans of oil in the back seat."

I stop, get out by the roadside and raise the hood. If Frank does have a gun, I think to myself, I'll give him a chance to use it now, while I still can get away. I go through the gestures of checking the oil, but all the time I am watching Frank out of the corner of my eye. In the moonlight I can see him fussing around inside his suitcoat, removing something shiny and fiddling with it.

Then I recognize a money clip and a thick roll of bills.

"Don't worry," Frank says, when I get back in the car. "I just wanted to threaten you, so you could tell Father Burkhart; maybe that way he'll let you stay."

When we reach the highway, I stop. The road stretches ahead straight and flat into the dark and there is no traffic in sight.

"Let's go back to the monastery, Frank," I plead. "We can talk things over in the morning."

"Hell, I won't do that."

"Please, Frank. They'll forgive you. You'll feel better tomorrow."

"No, I'm going." He opens the car door and stumbles out. He stands uncertainly on the pavement a moment.

"Come with me, Bill. We're friends. This is your last chance."

"No, I can't," I tell him.

"Good-bye, Bill," he says, reaching in to offer me his hand, "maybe you're a bigger man than I am." Then he starts lurching off down the highway.

"Take it easy, Frank, take care," I tell him. I sit there watching his dark figure weaving down the road into the darkness until he is out of sight. Then I turn around and head back, ready to face Father Burkhart.

When I get back, the door to the recreation room is still locked. I knock and call out my name, and finally Father Burkhart opens it cautiously. His face is pale, as I'm sure mine is. The others are huddled around a table at the back of the room and peer at me.

"Where is he?" Father Burkhart asks. "Has he gone?"

"Yes, he has, Father Burkhart." I stand in the doorway, afraid to go in, not knowing whether I am welcome or not.

"Where did you leave him?" he asks.

"I'd rather not say."

"You'll tell *me!*"

"No, I will not. If it harms Frank in any way, I won't tell you."

"I'll call the state police. They can stop a truck and put him on one headed for Texas. There's an abbey at Corpus Christi. He can go to Father Dave in the morning. They're old friends."

"I let him off at the state highway," I say.

Father Burkhart slams his fist down on the table. "Damn! I tried to make it easy for him. I said he could have coffee whenever he wanted it. I offered to put a coffee pot in the bakery. I told him he could come up to the kitchen whenever he wanted to."

Brother Patrick puffs on his pipe. "Frank always said, 'Let's go to Alejandro's, 'ave a drink, 'n' just listen to people talk.' But I never would."

Brother Vincent says, "We tried never to let Frank leave the monastery without one of us along. Tonight I should've tied him up with a length of clothesline, thrown him in the bathtub, and run some cold water over him. That would've sobered him up."

"He backed that bus through the wall of my print shop," Brother Thomas says. "He could've killed himself. He walked off with Father Burkhart's religious clothes and his clerical collar, too. Then I heard him banging and crashing around down here in the basement. He pulled out a lot of electrical wiring in the ceiling. The lights are out upstairs in the friary, so I can't tell what other damage he did, but he broke a lot of windows. And there's five-hundred dollars gone from the cash box in the bakery."

"My God," I say, remembering the clip and the roll of bills I saw in his hand.

"Father Burkhart gave him a key," Brother Thomas continues.

"He thought the responsibility would be good for him."

Father Burkhart breaks in. "Damn! We all knew he was an alcoholic. I could see he was working up to another drunk. It was bound to happen sooner or later. Well, we don't mind getting rid of Frank one bit." Then he turns to me. "You can go, too, anytime, Bill."

"I was planning on leaving right after you sent Father Bede away," I reply. "But I stayed around because I thought I could help Frank, by being a friend."

"No one can help Frank," Brother Thomas says.

"Nothing can ever excuse what he did tonight, but I think you're wrong," I say. "He has some good traits and Father Bede knows it. He understands Frank."

"Frank's a gyrovague."

"A what?"

"That's what Holy Father called them," Brother Thomas continues. "They're unstable monks who wander around from monastery to monastery, spend three days in this one, a week in another. We don't want that kind. We want to be left alone."

I glance at Brother Patrick, but he lowers his eyes. No one else speaks. I turn around and walk out and go back to my room.

All good things come to an end, but there are always new beginnings

Tonight is the first sleepless night since I arrived at the monastery. It is devastating, the loneliest moment of my life. My mind keeps going around and around, whether I am lying down or sitting on the edge of the bed.

Where is Frank now? Is he out there somewhere stumbling down the dark desert highway? Has he caught a ride? Or has he been arrested and is he in jail? I can't stop worrying about him.

There is a knock on my door. It is Brother Vincent. "Father's worried about you. He wants you to come over and sleep in a cell tonight. Frank might come back."

"That's very kind," I say, "but Frank wouldn't hurt me. Well, okay, I guess I will, Brother Vincent."

He leads me to a cell in the courtyard.

It is midnight. The cows are up in the yard again. I can hear their bells. Big Boy is no longer around to chase them off. Someone shot him. He dragged himself home with half his skull blown away. Brother Vincent didn't think there was enough left, and finished him with his .45.

Before I turn off the light, I reread the letter that arrived several days ago from Father Bede.

"I have interesting plans and hopes for the future that I long to discuss with you. I do every night beg God for strength to do good. To give up your life for Christ is to experience life to the fullest. The path will lead through difficulties and joys, sweat and tears, but also glorious adventure and inevitable conquest. To stay home, dear friend, is to miss the show."

All night I toss and turn and have dreams about Frank coming back and breaking down my door.

I am jarred awake from my restless dreams by a screeching, splintering noise. I sit bolt upright in bed, my heart hammering, not remembering where I am. It is the bell rope, hanging down through my cell to the basement below, rubbing against a loose, flapping floorboard near my bed as Brother Patrick tugs it.

I dress and go to Mass. It is still dark outside. The pews for the laity are empty and it is dim and cold.

Father Burkhart and the others are gathered in the choir near the altar. The place where Frank always stood, next to Patrick, is empty. After silent prayer, the chanting begins.

I had greatly admired Frank, his brains and muscles, his rugged good looks, his self-confidence, his ability to take care of himself, and his humor, too, his gentle side, his compassion, his willingness to listen.

But I had never seen Frank lose control before. It frightened me. Was this always a part of his life? Frank sought refuge at the monastery, brought his problems with him, and let his anger and frustration get the best of him, bringing chaos to the quiet life of the other monks. Father Bede was ousted, but he had left quietly, off on a new adventure, still believing in himself and in what he was trying to do.

Father Bede is gone and so is Frank.

Father Burkhart says Mass. Suddenly I look up and see one of Frank's kittens standing in the doorway of the vestry. She comes in, stretches, peers around, and then jumps up on the step behind Father Burkhart, who is facing the altar, and begins playing with the lace hem of the back of the alb. She gets a claw hooked in the material and rolls over on her back and bicycles with her hind legs to free it. Once she disappears entirely under Father's robes. When he steps forward with the cat still caught, his robe balloons out in back like a tent. Brother Patrick spots her. He steps out of the choir, genuflects, crosses himself, snatches her up and puts her out. Father Burkhart never knew what happened. Seeing Frank's cat makes me feel anguish: Where is Frank? Where did he go last night? I pray that no harm has come to him. I know I'll never see him again.

I can't bear to stay any longer. My car is already loaded. Before Mass is over I slip out quietly. I don't want to say good-bye.

The road to Carlsbad stretches ahead. Behind me are the distant mountain pines and snow-covered passes of the Guadalupes.

Over and over I relive my days at the monastery. Father Bede, Deaf Don, Brother Patrick, Father Alfonse, Father Burkhart—and Big Boy, buried down in the pasture where he loved to romp. And Martha: I miss her so much it is too painful to think about, but I will write to her as soon as I am settled. Then my thoughts return to Frank. What forces, I wonder, truly shape a man's life? And was my stay at the monastery the result of Divine Causality, as Father Bede had said, or was it mere chance? Chance, most likely. But I know now that a life without Christ would be lonely and unbearable.

Light snow fell during the night but it is already melting under the bright sun. The oil stick is level, Carlsbad lies in the distance, the roads are open and so am I, open with hope to the challenge of the unknown.